HORSE-DRAWN DAYS

HORSE-DRAWN DAYS

A Century of Farming with Horses

JERRY APPS

WISCONSIN HISTORICAL SOCIETY PRESS

Published by the Wisconsin Historical Society Press
Publishers since 1855

Text © 2010 by Jerold W. Apps

Publication of this book was made possible in part by a grant from the Alice E. Smith fellowship fund.

wisconsin**history**.org

Frontmatter photo credits: page ii, Old World Wisconsin historic site / Wisconsin Historical Society; page v, WHi Image ID 11849; page vi, WHi Image ID 3560

Photographs identified with WHi or WHS are from the Society's collections; address requests to reproduce these photos to the Visual Materials Archivist at the Wisconsin Historical Society, 816 State Street, Madison, WI 53706.

Printed in the United States of America
Designed by Steve Biel

14 13 12 11 10   1 2 3 4 5

Library of Congress Cataloging-in-Publication Data

Apps, Jerold W., 1934-
  Horse-drawn days: a century of farming with horses / Jerry Apps.—1st ed.
    p. cm.
  Includes bibliographical references and index.
  ISBN 978-0-87020-445-6 (pbk. : alk. paper) 1. Draft horses—United States—History. 2. Horse-drawn vehicles—United States—History. 3. Farm life—United States—History. 4. Farm life—Middle West—History. 5. Agriculture. I. Title.
  SF311.3.U6A77 2010
  636.1'509775—dc22
                        2009037494

*To all the farmers
who grew up driving horses
and will forever love them*

EUREKA

EUREKA MOWER CO. TOWANDA, PA.

CONTENTS

ACKNOWLEDGMENTS

Many people helped me with this book. I want to thank all who sent me stories about their memories of working with horses, some including photos. Allen Schroeder, site director for the Wisconsin Historical Society's Stonefield in Cassville, gave me easy access to the vast collection of horse-drawn farm machinery there. My son Steve provided many of the photographs for the book. The Wisconsin Historical Society Archives was an invaluable source of farm machinery photographs and other images.

As she does with all my books, my wife, Ruth, read several drafts of the manuscript. She has the uncanny ability to raise the question, "What does this mean?" when I think something is perfectly clear. And finally, I can't say enough about Kate Thompson, my editor at the Wisconsin Historical Society Press. She is a stickler for logic and detail and knows how to take my sometimes-obtuse organization of material and make it readable.

Many other people helped as well, and I thank each of them. Book writing, although seemingly a solitary activity, requires the assistance of many.

With a trusty team and a high-wheeled wagon, a farmer shows off his load of hay on its way to the barn. For many Wisconsin farmers, haying season began in late June and continued into early August. (WHI IMAGE ID 53641)

INTRODUCTION

When I was a kid growing up on a central Wisconsin farm during World War II, everyone in our rural community farmed with horses. A few continued using horses long after that. When my dad bought a tractor in 1945, he kept the team. "One thing about horses, no matter how cold it is, they always start," he said with a big smile. That's more than could be said about our shiny new Farmall tractor. It sat like a block of ice when the temperature dipped to twenty below zero, refusing to move.

I learned how to drive horses at an early age, seven or eight. I can't say I enjoyed it. The horses were huge, weighing nearly a ton each. I was afraid they'd step on my feet— and sometimes they did. I don't think they cared much for me, either. They were my dad's team, and the horses would do anything for him; they respected him, they listened to him, and I believe they enjoyed his company. I was more of a bother, something akin to the horseflies that sometimes buzzed around their ears.

I learned early, though, that our team was important on our farm, as important as our family, our farm dog, the barn, even the land itself. The team did everything, from hauling manure in the spring, plowing, disking, and cutting hay and grain, to pulling a bundle wagon from neighbor to neighbor during threshing season. Without the horses, we couldn't work the farm.

In *Horse-Drawn Days* I hope to preserve that era when horses were a vital part of our everyday lives. In these pages I examine the horse's importance to humans, from the animal's earliest history through the second agricultural revolution, when electricity replaced oil lamps and lanterns, hybrid seed and commercial fertilizers became commonplace, and tractors took over for horses. And, drawing on my memories and those of fellow horse farmers, I have tried to capture what it was like farming with horses through all four seasons, from spring plowing to toting stove wood out of the woodlot when snow came up to the horses' bellies.

Today, hundreds of farmers and former farmers gather at antique tractor shows and gaze at those first cast-iron machines with awe and nostalgia. Yet there was a time in the history of our land when horses garnered even more respect. Both horses and tractors

With the arrival of spring, the farmer and team spent many hours preparing the soil and planting crops. Sometimes junior came along for the ride as Dad drove the team on a smoothing drag, as on this farm near Thiensville, Wisconsin, 1934. (WHI IMAGE ID 8289)

pulled farm implements. But horses, of course, are fundamentally different. They are living creatures, with personalities and faults, just like the farmers who cared for them day in and day out, year after year. When an old tractor died, no one grieved its going. But when an old horse died, the family shed many tears, for the animal had been a part of the family and a friend. For some bachelor farmers, horses were the only friends they had.

Horses played a major role in this country's earliest history and remained a vital force in its development until the mid-twentieth century. In recent years, in the face of modern agricultural technology, the trusty draft horse has mostly been forgotten. But horses deserve to be remembered for their contributions to the development of farming—and to the development of our country. At one time draft horses were everywhere, on farms, in small towns, and in the largest of cities. In many ways, and for a hundred years, draft horses were the drivers of the economy, while also contributing to social life.

PART I

A Time for Horses

From pioneer days in America until World War II, horses pulled the plows, hauled the heavy wagons, and transported people from here to there. They pulled the buggies for grocery shopping and courting, for going to church and stopping at the saloon. They did the work that automobiles, trucks, and tractors do today, and they did it quietly, with no dependence on foreign oil to keep them going and no computer chips to monitor their behavior. No exhaust fumes polluted the air, either, if you can disregard the smell of a little horse manure left in their wake. No screeching of tires and roaring of engines, although on occasion harsh words spilled from a driver bumped by another less careful one. To the best of my knowledge, no horseman was ever pulled over for drunken driving. When the driver became incapacitated, the horse took over, bringing the over-imbiber home, often without his knowledge.

For many years it was a world of horses. People in town and country alike owned them and depended on them. Behind most houses in towns and villages was a little horse barn, and every town, large and small, had a livery stable where one could rent a horse and buggy. Horses pulled fire engines, hauled milk delivery wagons, and carried rural mail carriers along their routes. Breweries had their own horses to haul the massive barrels of beer to the taverns. A dray service—today's trucking business—was available in most towns, its teams and wagons available to haul merchandise from the railroad station to the various merchants and to transport train travelers to the town's hotels and boarding houses.

As late as 1919, after the first automobiles had made their appearance, publications such as *The Old Farmer's Almanac* continued to encourage the use of horses for transportation, recognizing both the benefits and the challenges:

> *There are still, happily, many folks who take more solid comfort to riding behind a good horse than they do in rushing through the country in an automobile. They relish the sociability that is impossible when the road ahead must be watched closely and constantly, and they like the slow pace that affords a chance to see the surroundings. But there is not much opportunity for such to take pleasure in riding over the slippery, motor-crowded main roads; they must perforce keep to the side and less frequented highways.*[1]

The century 1850 through 1950 was a time for horses, when these noble creatures performed nearly all the tasks that motorized vehicles do today. The era of the horse was a slower time in America, a time for thinking, for fully experiencing one's surroundings, and for close connections between people and animals.

Previous spread:
From early settlement days to the mid-twentieth century, farmers depended on horses for transportation and, by the 1830s, for much of the heavy work on the farm. In this circa 1878 photo, a Wisconsin farm family shows off their team and carriage.
(WHI IMAGE ID 26439)

As villages and cities organized, each of them had one or more livery stables where horses could be rented and sometimes boarded. Livery stables, like this one in Sheboygan, circa 1892, were akin to the car rental offices we know today. (WHI IMAGE ID 40886)

HORSES IN OUR LANGUAGE

Horse expressions still permeate our language, reflecting the time when horses played a central role in our lives:

You can lead a horse to water, but you can't make him drink. *People don't always take advantage of a good opportunity.*

Get off your high horse. *Act like an ordinary person.*

Quit horsing around. *Behave yourself.*

Don't put the cart before the horse. *First things first.*

Don't switch horses in midstream. *Know when to change plans.*

He supported a dark horse candidate. *He supported someone not expected to win.*

Hold your horses. *Stop, wait, take your time. This comes from the days of circus parades, when horse owners were warned, "The elephants are coming, hold your horses."*

She heard it straight from the horse's mouth. *She heard something directly from a dependable source.*

He was beating a dead horse. *He was continuing to support a worthless idea.*

She eats like a horse. *She eats a lot.*

He works like a horse. *He works hard.*

She backed the wrong horse. *She backed a losing candidate. This is often used in politics.*

That's a horse of a different color. *That is a situation different from what was expected.*

It was a one-horse town. *It was a small town where not much happens.*

He has horse sense. *He has common sense.*

She knows how to horse trade. *She knows how to bargain skillfully.*

Don't look a gift horse in the mouth. *Don't complain about a gift or a good opportunity.*

The Davies and Thomas families pause from their work at James Davies's farm near Wild Rose, Wisconsin, circa 1900.
(WHI IMAGE ID 55558)

Early steam fire engines, like this one in Milwaukee, circa 1900, were horse drawn. Along with the firefighters, fire stations housed the teams, which were selected for their speed and endurance.
(WHI IMAGE ID 5029)

Stagecoaches provided an important means of transportation in the mid-nineteenth century. This horse-drawn stagecoach operated between Sparta and Eau Claire, Wisconsin, in the late 1850s and 1860s.
(WHI IMAGE ID 43790)

1

A BRIEF HISTORY OF THE HORSE

Cave paintings in France and Spain believed to have been rendered about fifteen thousand years ago include pictures of horses. At that time people hunted horses for their meat and hides. Evidence unearthed in northern Europe suggests that humans domesticated horses for the first time about six thousand years ago. People used these first domesticated horses primarily as pack animals; later they harnessed and hitched the horses to wheeled carts and chariots. By 1000 BC horses were used extensively in wars, knights in armor riding heavy steeds into battle.

Christopher Columbus is credited with bringing horses to the New World in 1493. By that time the creatures had been extinct for thousands of years in what is now North America.

Spanish explorers also brought horses to North America in the 1500s.[1] The horse became the means for long-distance travel and began playing important roles in industry and in agriculture.[2]

Early Farming Practices

For thousand of years humans across the globe lived by hunting and gathering. People were constantly on the move, foraging food from the countryside and hunting wild game. Farming—growing crops and domesticating animals—meant staying in one place, a dramatic change for people who enjoyed and depended on moving from one area to another throughout the year. Many generations passed before most hunters and gatherers became farmers. Some never did.

Historians claim the earliest farmers lived some ten thousand years ago in what is now Turkey and the Middle East. These farmers grew varieties of our present-day wheat, barley, and peas. They had few tools for working the soil, planting seeds, and harvesting crops. They used a primitive plow, which may have been as simple as a forked stick,

An 1893 Johnson Harvester Company catalog depicted a startled Christopher Columbus gazing down at a horse-drawn reaper and mused over "what Columbus would see now."
(WHI IMAGE ID 11856)

to loosen the soil prior to planting. About AD 1000 some farmers began replacing this simple device (still common today in some underdeveloped countries) with a plow that cut the sod and turned it over by means of a strip of curved material called a moldboard. This new, heavier plow worked best when pulled by an animal such as an ox.

For centuries farming changed little. Farmers labored in their fields, planting crops, weeding, and harvesting. The work was hard, and the yields were meager. When growing wheat, for instance, farmers turned the soil with a primitive plow, smoothed it with a simple homemade device such as a smoothing drag, sowed the seeds by hand, harvested the crop with a homemade sickle, and threshed the grain with a flail. Even though some improvements were made in the construction of plows, no substantial advancement occurred in crop varieties or in farm machinery until the 1700s.[3] But these procedures began to change and adapt as settlers moved west.

By the time pioneers began arriving in the Midwest in the late 1830s, the breaking plow was the tool of choice for turning the heavy prairie soils in preparation for planting wheat. The more primitive plows that farmers had used in New England did not work well where the prairie grasses grew tall and the soil contained more clay. (For more detail about plows, see page 94.)

Wooden-beamed breaking plows like this one, with a long, sweeping moldboard and pulled by several teams of oxen, turned much of the virgin soil of the Midwest. Both the moldboard and plow point were made of polished steel, which allowed the plow to move easily through the heavy midwestern soils.
(PHOTO BY STEVE APPS, TAKEN AT STONEFIELD HISTORIC SITE)

OXEN

Well into the mid-1800s, oxen were widely used for the heavy work on midwestern farms. Red Durham became the breed of choice, as they gave milk, provided power, and could be used for meat. A Red Durham ox might weigh 1,500 pounds or more.

From early settlement years until the mid-1800s, farmers depended on oxen to do the heavy work around the farm: plowing, hauling logs, and pulling heavy wagonloads. Here a yoke of oxen pulls a high-wheeled wagon near Black River Falls, Wisconsin, date unknown. (WHI IMAGE ID 41942)

Oxen do not move quickly. One of the popular jokes in the 1800s was that oxen could do everything better than horses—except getting the farmer to church. If you started out for church on a Sunday morning, you would probably arrive the following Tuesday.

In 1930 a fellow with the unusual name of Tap Snilloc told a writer for the *Stevens Point Journal* about his grandfather's use of oxen:

When I was a youngster my grandfather lived on a farm in the town of Almond [Portage County] and it was his custom to come to the city [Stevens Point] in the fall and spring of the year, to do his semi-annual trading. He and my grandmother would start from the old farm early in the morning on the cumbersome journey to the county seat, behind the plodding faithful yoke of oxen, named Buck and Bright. The journey occupied the greater part of the day and when they finally reached our home they were ready for the customary cup of tea that mother always brewed on the arrival of this kindly old couple. After resting for the night they started out to do the trading for the family back on the farm. Their purchases generally consisted of a barrel of pork, flour, sugar, coffee, tea and calicos, ginghams and muslin cloth to make into dresses for the girls, and other household necessities, not omitting a generous supply of medicinal remedies every farmhouse carried in case of need. These purchases took up the greater part of the second day, and on the morning of the third, they loaded up their little store of provisions, and with Godspeed from our family, would start on the return journey to the home farm. This semi-annual trek to the city occupied three days and I cite this fact to emphasize the cumbersome methods the pioneers of the county encountered in their journeys to the trading points.[1]

(continued on next page)

OXEN

(continued from page 9)

Lars P. Larson, who arrived in Wisconsin from Norway in 1857 when he was ten years old, recalled some of his adventures driving oxen. One of his jobs, when he was but fourteen, was driving a load of wheat from Ettrick to Trempealeau, a distance of twenty-one miles. It was a two-day trip. Larson described the experience this way:

We would start at 4 o'clock in the morning and drive to a hollow near what is now the Herbert farm, or to one just beyond on the Salsman. There were always a number of teams. The oxen would be picketed for the

night, then we would build a campfire. After supper there would be story-telling, and sometimes songs, before we rolled into our blankets. The next day we would pull into Trempealeau and deliver our wheat to the docks.[2]

NOTES

1. Tap Snilloc, "Buck and Bright, Faithful Oxen, Helped Pioneer Carve Out Farms," *Antigo Daily Journal*, April 2, 1930. Reprinted from *Stevens Point Journal*.

2. "Back to the Covered Wagon and Oxen," *Galesville Republican*, June 12, 1930.

NOTES FROM
The Horse Barn

While many Wisconsin settlers might have wanted to farm with horses, not all could afford them. In Vernon County in 1856, a yoke of oxen cost from $100 to $150, while a single horse cost between $100 and $200.[5]

At the same time, farmers were finding they could do considerably more work with horses than with oxen. A horse's gait is about twice as fast as that of oxen, and horses are more maneuverable. As more mechanized and complicated farm equipment such as the reaper began emerging, horses provided the steady, constant speed such equipment required.[4]

The Industrial Revolution

The industrial revolution that began in the textile industry in Great Britain in the late 1700s and continued into the mid-1800s, spreading across Europe and North America, led to a dramatic shift from the dependence on homegrown artisans. With the mechanization of labor and the increased reliance on coal and water power, factories soon began manufacturing the products of the blacksmith, wagonmaker, and harness shop. These changes in turn had a great effect on farming, as a succession of machines capable of speeding farmwork emerged and animal power began replacing human power on the farm. Early rural sociologist Charles Galpin wrote:

The machine is profoundly affecting the farmer's physical and mental life, as it is all human life. With every advance in machine power for the farmstead, both in the house and on the land, a shift occurs in the strain upon the farm family. . . . As the hoe-man becomes obsolete and the farm engineer takes his place, the main typical task of the farmstead shifts its burden from the back of the peasant to the fingers and eyes of the rural mechanician.[6]

Galpin went on to predict that the farmer, with less need for heavy physical work, would have more time for the "employment of his hereditary intellectual mechanism, and a consequent intellectual life."[7] Galpin failed to recognize that farmwork would continue to present both physical and mental challenges for many years to come. How many farmers of the era found time for an "intellectual life" remains an unanswered question.

Patents protected many of the new machines, which helped encourage inventors. Unfortunately, patent infringement occurred often and led to many court battles. Nevertheless, small entrepreneurial businesses sprang up throughout the East and Midwest. Their owners—some of them former blacksmiths, many of them once farmers, and all of them possessing great imagination and ingenuity—developed dozens of new machines. Of course, many of these machines and shops failed, but a considerable number succeeded. The companies most familiar to people today, such as John Deere, McCormick, Deering, and Case, made their fortunes developing horse-drawn farm implements: plows, cultivators, grain drills, corn planters, disk harrows, reapers, corn binders, horse-powered threshing machines, and hay presses.

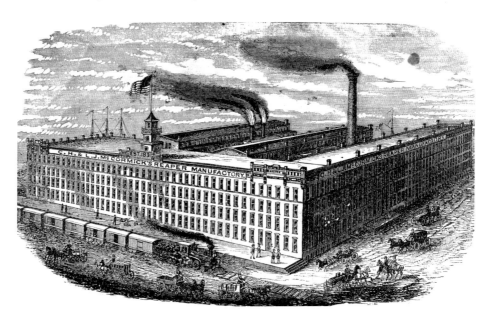

By the mid- to late 1800s, huge farm machinery manufacturing plants were springing up around the country. After the Chicago fire of 1871 destroyed an earlier plant, the McCormick Company built this one.
(WHI IMAGE ID 24887)

HORSEPOWER

A team of well-muscled draft horses pulls a one-bottom walking plow at Wade House historic site in Greenbush, Wisconsin. Horse power had replaced oxen power by the mid-1800s. (WADE HOUSE HISTORIC SITE / WISCONSIN HISTORICAL SOCIETY)

Many of us bandy about the term *horsepower* no matter if we're talking about automobiles or airplane engines: "How much horsepower does that pickup have, anyway?"

The term *horsepower* didn't even exist until inventors developed machines that did work similar to what a horse might do. When horses provided most of the power on farms and in urban centers, everyone knew what a horse could or could not do, so no one talked about horsepower as a technical

term for measurement. Eighteenth-century inventor James Watt is credited with developing the term. Seeking a clever way to advertise his patented steam engines, Watt compared the power of his new invention to the power of a horse. (Note that the unit of power called a watt—named for Watt, of course—is equal to 1/746 of one horsepower.)

It's a confusing concept. You would think "one horsepower" equals the work one horse can do. But could an automobile with 200 horsepower hold

HORSEPOWER

an engine that equals the power of 200 horses? And what about the difference in the size of horses? Surely a big horse weighing a ton or more can pull more than one weighing half that much.

Technically, horsepower is defined as *the power needed to lift 550 pounds off the ground in one second.* Here's another, more evocative way of illustrating horsepower: "If a horse is walking 2.5 miles an hour and exerting a steady pull on his traces [tugs] of 150 pounds, the effective energy which he develops is . . . one horsepower."[1]

So, how much can a horse pull? Frank Morrison, a longtime Cornell University professor of animal science, has explained, "At steady and continuous work for 10 hours a day, the pull (or draft) for a horse should not be more than one-eighth to one-tenth its weight. . . . A 1,600 pound horse should not be required to exert an average pull of more than 160 to 200 pounds."[2]

However, draft horses have tremendous reserve power. A good team is usually capable of pulling ten times its normal rate, sometimes pulling as much as what the team itself weighs. Working horses employ this reserve power often. When a team is hitched to a loaded wagon, it takes more than ten times more pull to start the wagon moving than to keep it moving (remember inertia?). And reserve power is necessary when going up hills and moving over uneven terrain.

Generally speaking, the larger the horse, the more it can pull. But many other factors affect a horse's pulling ability. Even the disposition of the

A farmer shows off his Percheron colt at the Wisconsin State Fair, circa 1900. The Percheron became one of the most popular draft horse breeds for farmwork. (WHI IMAGE ID 33797)

driver is a factor. A team will not give a high-strung driver its best performance. A poor-fitting harness, especially a loose collar, will diminish a horse's pulling capacity. Poorly shod horses can also generally pull less than those that are properly shod. An interesting aside: an ox can pull about as heavy a load as a horse of the same weight, but at two-thirds the speed.[3]

NOTES

1. J. Brownlee Davidson and Leon Wilson Chase, *Farm Machinery: Practical Hints for Handy-men* (Guilford, CT: The Lyons Press, 1999), 11.

2. Frank B. Morrison, *Feeds and Feeding* (Ithaca, NY: The Morrison Publishing Company, 1956), 821.

3. Ibid., 821–823.

THE HOMESTEAD ACT OF 1862

2:37- Congress Session II 1862

Chapter LXXV.—*An Act to secure Homesteads to actual Settlers on the Public Domain. Be it enacted by the Senate and House of Representatives of the United States of America in Congress assembled, that any person who is the head of a family, or who has arrived at the age of twenty-one years, and is a citizen of the United States, or who shall have filed his declaration of intention to become such, as required by the naturalization laws of the United States, and who has never borne arms against the United States Government or given aid and comfort to its enemies, shall, from and after the first January, eighteen hundred and sixty-three, be entitled to enter one quarter section or a less quantity of unappropriated public lands, . . .*

Entrepreneurs flourished in the years following the Civil War with the passage of the 1862 Homestead Act legislation. Signed into law by Abraham Lincoln on May 20, 1862, the Homestead Act turned over 270 million acres of public domain land to private citizens. The law remained in effect until it was repealed in 1976, with some provisions for homesteading continuing in Alaska until 1986.

A homesteader had to be the head of a household or twenty-one years old in order to claim up to a 160-acre parcel of land. Both women and men could apply, and they need only pay a ten dollar filing fee and two dollar commission to the land agent to obtain the land. The new landholder had five years to "prove up," meaning he or she had to build a cabin, farm the land, and live on the property. At the end of five years, the homesteader paid an additional six dollar fee and received the patent for the land, which meant full ownership, no strings attached.[8]

Also during the post–Civil War years, steam power came into its own. Steamboats moved up and down the Mississippi, Ohio, and other major rivers. Steam locomotives hauled passengers and cargo as crews laid rails at ever-increasing rates. As early as 1868, the first steam tractors began appearing. These cumbersome giants weighed tons, had a great appetite for fuel, and belched out a smelly plume of gray-black smoke. Many of these behemoths were so heavy they couldn't move themselves; when they tried to do farmwork such as plowing, they became hopelessly stuck. Horse-drawn equipment continued to excel at farmwork, especially plowing, planting, cultivating, and harvesting crops. But for stationary tasks, such as powering a threshing machine, the steam tractor quickly replaced the horse-powered machines.

With innovations in manufacturing, horse-drawn equipment became larger—bigger plows, wider disk harrows, grain binders that would cut more grain. Larger equipment required bigger horses, and more of them. Horse dealers began importing large draft horse breeds from Europe, such as Percherons, Belgians, Clydesdales, Shires, and Suffolks. By 1900 the average-sized workhorse had increased in weight from twelve hundred or fourteen hundred pounds to as much as a ton.[9]

Many farmers still preferred the slow, plodding, but strong oxen to pull their farm implements. These animals ate less than horses and could themselves be eaten when they were no longer useful as draft animals. But for all their advantages, oxen were pitifully slow.[10] Machinery manufacturers designed their machines for horses, not oxen. And with cities growing larger, the demand for draft horses increased there just as on the farm. Urban draft horses pulled beer and milk wagons, hauled people from train depots to hotels, and moved goods throughout these emerging metropolitan areas. From 1900 to 1910 the number of draft horses in the United States increased from 13 million to 23 million. By 1919 U.S. horse numbers would reach an all-time high, nearly 26 million.[11]

Steam tractors began appearing on Wisconsin farms in the late 1800s. They were slow and clumsy and most suited to powering machines such as grain separators. In this circa 1900 photo, taken near Ogema, Wisconsin, a steam tractor runs a threshing machine.
(WHI IMAGE ID 41752)

For many farmers, their horses were as much a part of the family as was the family dog.

(WHI IMAGE ID 43569)

In villages and cities, horses delivered milk and other goods daily. This photo, taken in Madison in 1934, shows a rubber-tired milk wagon making its rounds.

(WHI IMAGE ID 25908)

The Agricultural Revolution

Along with the invention and popularization of horse-drawn farm implements and machinery, several other factors led to the start of an agricultural revolution in the mid-1800s. Major forces included the movement of industry from farms and small towns to factories; a liberal land policy (including the Homestead Act) that moved thousands of acres of land from the public domain into private ownership; and the extension and development of transportation facilities, including the rapid expansion of railroads, the development of canals, riverboat shipping, Great Lakes steamboat shipping, and the beginning of improved roads (although it would be years before good farm-to-market roads became common). Railroads grew at an unbelievable rate. In 1860 the United States had 30,000 miles of railroad, most of it in the northeastern states. By 1920 the nation boasted 253,000 miles of rails covering most of the country.[12] With better transportation, the number of farmers' markets grew, and those firms manufacturing farm implements and equipment could send their products to their customers more easily.

With the agricultural revolution came the development of agencies and organizations with the purpose of promoting scientific agriculture and distributing information about farming. Agricultural societies, which had their roots in the Northeast, spread west with the settlers. These societies, of and for farmers, had both local and state representation. A Wisconsin agricultural society was organized in 1851, but by that time nine county societies were already active.[13]

In 1862, the same year he signed the Homestead Act, President Lincoln created the United States Department of Agriculture (USDA) and signed legislation to finance land-grant universities. Both the USDA and the land-grant institutions conducted scientific agricultural research and distributed information to farmers for improving farming. A host of periodicals carried information about improving farming strategies and displayed ads by machinery manufacturers proclaiming the benefits of purchasing a particular implement.

The end of the Civil War in 1865 brought monumental changes in U.S. farming practices. Horses and horse-drawn equipment and machinery were the centerpiece of a sea change in how farmers produced food and fiber in this country. Farmers would continue to depend on horses until the next agricultural revolution (1945–1960), when tractors would replace these faithful servants and most horse-drawn machinery would be left to rust on the hillside behind the barn.

In 1867 Wisconsin had 206,000 horses; by 1900 the number had grown to 536,000. The number of horses in the state rose to a pinnacle of 748,000 in 1915. In that year these horses had an average value of $131 each, up from $62 in 1900. From 1900 to

NOTES FROM

The Horse Barn

The first humane societies in the United States focused much of their efforts on the welfare of horses and livestock. The work of Henry Bergh, founder of the American Society for the Prevention of Cruelty to Animals in 1866, led to the first ambulance for injured horses, the invention of a horse-rescue sling, and a fresh drinking water supply for the horses that pulled carts and streetcars in New York City.[14]

Horses were used extensively in building railroads, doing such work as grading roadbeds and even hauling locomotives and cars over land. These horses are pulling a loco- motive from Lone Rock to Richland Center during construction of the Pine River and Stevens Point Railroad, 1875.
(WHI IMAGE ID 24557)

1915, the number of horses per farm also increased: in 1900, 91 percent of Wisconsin farms used horses; in 1915, 94 percent did. In that year each Wisconsin farm had, on average, slightly fewer than four horses. [15]

As the production of farm machinery moved from small-town blacksmith and woodworking shops to factories in major urban centers, informing potential customers became more difficult. Elaborate marketing and advertising schemes quickly emerged. Publicity and advertising, of course, were not new ideas. The circus—from the little-known one-ring affairs to the gigantic shows such as the Ringling Brothers—had introduced rural and urban people alike to advertising decades earlier. But while circus advertising almost always included a certain amount of exaggeration—and sometimes outright lies—farm machinery manufacturers found that hyperbole and deception usually backfired. You might fool a farmer once, but not a second time. Besides, if a machine failed to meet its promises, the disgruntled farmer was sure to let his neighbors and anyone else who would listen know about it.

The field demonstration became a popular way to promote farm equipment. Inventor Cyrus McCormick (see page 135) sent sales reps into the wheat-growing country of the Midwest to show farmers exactly how his McCormick reaper functioned. It was one thing for a farmer to read an ad about the reaper in the newspaper or a farm periodical, but it was quite another to see the machine operate. The old saw "Seeing is believing" held true. Imagine the farmer who has never known another way to harvest wheat than cutting it by hand with a cradle, binding it by hand, standing the bound wheat bundles into grain shocks to dry, and threshing the dried shocks by hand with a flail. Now, the farmer hears about this new contraption, pulled by a team of horses, that will cut the wheat. He can't image such a machine could even be possible—until a McCormick salesperson arrives at a neighbor's farm and cuts a few acres of wheat in a couple of hours.

The farmer has already decided to give the reaper a try when he learns the price—many times more than the cost of a new cradle. But McCormick has an answer for this sales challenge: the monthly payment plan. This was a new and appealing idea, and Cyrus McCormick, one of the first to use the practice, sold thousands of reapers this way. (The plan also provided the McCormick Company many headaches when it came time to collect payments from farmers down on their luck, facing a drought, or offering a hundred other reasons why they couldn't make their payment.)

Agricultural fairs also were popular venues for showing off both horses and new farm machines. The first county fair in Wisconsin was held in Kenosha County in 1850; by the 1860s the state boasted thirty county fairs. Wisconsin's first state fair ran the first two days of October 1851 on the shores of the Rock River in Janesville. Rufus King, owner and editor of the *Milwaukee Sentinel*, wrote a flowery report of the exposition, including a description of the fairgrounds: "In the open space between these centre pieces and the cattle stands on the sides, there is ample room for exhibition

As the farm machinery business moved from blacksmith shop to factory, the emerging manufacturers used carefully designed posters to lure potential buyers to their products. By 1871 the Dodge and Stevenson Manufacturing Company of Auburn, New York, was one of many companies manufacturing reapers. (WHI IMAGE ID 3559)

Farmers are practical, frugal people. Reaper manufacturers set up demonstrations so farmers could see firsthand how various reapers performed in field conditions. Farmers had used their trusty and inexpensive cradles for years to harvest their grain. They wanted to make sure they were making the right decision when they purchased their first reapers.
(WHI IMAGE ID 44832)

and trial of all sorts of agricultural implements, as well as the display of single and matched horses."[17]

Agricultural fairs provided an excellent means for improving the quality of agricultural enterprises, as farmers had a chance to see firsthand, and compare, a lineup of corn planters, manure spreaders, disk harrows, farm wagons, and other farm machinery from several manufacturers. They could talk to the salespeople and to other farmers who had used a particular machine, becoming quite well informed before they decided what to purchase.

Plowing contests provided farmers another way to learn about various styles of plows and have some competitive fun at the same time. At Wisconsin's first state fair, ten farmers competed in a plowing contest, eight with horses and two with oxen. There is no record of the plows' manufacturers or who won the contest.[18]

By the 1860s manufacturers had established local dealerships in most agricultural communities. A farmer needed only to travel to a nearby town and find a John Deere, a McCormick, or some other well-known brand. The local dealer not only sold new equipment but also taught farmers how to use it, kept an inventory of spare parts, and maintained a trained staff to repair broken or worn-out machinery.

Some farm equipment manufacturers, especially the smaller ones, prided themselves on selling directly to farmers, bypassing the dealers and middlemen. They advertised heavily in the farm papers and boasted about how they kept their prices down by selling direct. For instance, the Wilber H. Murray manufacturing company of Cincinnati, Ohio, ran quarter-page ads like this one in farm papers:

> *Four years ago we began selling our Murray Buggies direct to the consumer, barring out all Middlemen in the shape of the Dealer and the Agent, and giving the consumers*

Agricultural fairs became popular venues for farmers to see new machinery, examine blue-ribbon horses, and compare notes with fellow farmers. Wisconsin Agricultural Society Fair, 1858.
(WHI IMAGE ID 24752)

themselves the benefits of the immense profits heretofore squeezed and coaxed out of them by that class of men. We were fully convinced that by selling at first cost to the consumer direct, and by giving them the most substantial, the newest styles and the best finished work that could be produced, we would be eminently successful.

What has been the result of our four years' work in reforming the Buggy and Harness business of the country? The result is simply this—that today our name is the criterion of quality and low prices. Our Murray Buggies and Harness are more widely used than any three makes in the whole country. Murray Buggy: $55.95, Harness: $5.95.[19]

The truth of these claims is unknown, but the ad certainly appealed to a farmer who always was a bit skeptical of the "middleman" and enjoyed the opportunity to work directly with the manufacturer. Of course, the farmer missed all the advantages of working with a local dealer, especially one who provided parts and repair service.

However the farmer obtained it, this new machinery was designed to be powered by horses. Indeed, the American agricultural revolution was fueled by the labor of the mighty draft horse.

Plowing with a team and a sulky plow at Old World Wisconsin historic site, near Eagle. With the introduction of the sulky plow, farmers could ride as they steered their team of draft horses across a field.

2

DRAFT HORSES AND THEIR EQUIPMENT

Before the 1830s few draft horses could be found in the United States. Farmers depended on oxen for plowing, tilling the soil, and hauling heavy loads with a wagon. Carriage horses, especially the Morgan horse, became extremely popular in the late 1700s and early 1800s. At fourteen to fifteen hands tall and weighing between 950 and 1,150 pounds, the Morgan horse is an American original, tracing back to a stallion named Figure owned by Vermont schoolmaster and composer Justin Morgan. The little bay stallion left many sons and daughters, and the breed became known as Justin Morgan's horse, or simply Morgan. The Morgan breed horses became popular for their versatility, capable of doing relatively heavy farmwork and serving as saddle and carriage horses.

Although never as popular as horses for farmwork, especially in the Midwest, mules also did their share of work as draft animals. A cross between a female horse and a male donkey, a mule has longer ears than a horse, a Roman nose, and a scant tail and mane. Mules weigh between 600 and 1,600 pounds and stand between fourteen and seventeen hands tall. They are sterile and will not reproduce, but they are hardy, adapt well to most climates, and are dependable draft animals.

Mules were often used to pull farm equipment in the South. This Clarksdale, Mississippi, plantation worker drives a team of mules on a planter, 1928. (WHI IMAGE ID 23692)

Draft Horse Breeds

The common draft horse breeds include Percheron, Belgian, Clydesdale, Suffolk, and Shire. Farmers most often used Percherons and Belgians for farmwork but owned other breeds as well. Often the owner's preference determined what breed of horse he or she owned and worked. Breeders commonly cross-bred horses, meaning a horse might be part Percheron and part Belgian. Sometimes an excellent horse in every way had a totally unknown heritage.

Eighteen-year-old Otto Holzschuh shows off his Percheron in front of J. Zierer's photo shop in Plymouth, Wisconsin, 1902. (PHOTO COURTESY OF JEAN HOLZSCHUH SWEET)

Belgian. Country of origin: Belgium. Belgian horses have relatively short legs and wide, muscular, compact bodies. Their heads are square and their necks short. They generally weigh between 1,600 and 2,400 pounds.

Clydesdale. Country of origin: Scotland. Distinctive features include relatively long legs with good action (moving easily, with little effort). They weigh between 1,500 and 2,200 pounds. The breed has a history of use in the brewing industry. The brewer Anheuser-Busch continues to use an eight-horse Clydesdale hitch to advertise its product.

Percheron. Country of origin: France. Percherons were introduced to the United States in the 1830s. They weigh between 1,600 and 2,200 pounds. Their distinctive features include a strong yet well-proportioned neck. They are intelligent and have a pleasant temperament. Before railroads, many were used as stagecoach horses and for hauling freight. Later, Percheron breeders developed a larger, heavy horse more suited for heavy farmwork. The railroad circuses, including the Ringling Brothers, preferred Percherons because they were small enough to fit easily in railcars for moving from city to city, strong enough to pull heavy circus wagons, and docile enough so crowds and noise wouldn't frighten them.

Shire. Country of origin: England. The Shire is the largest of the draft horse breeds, weighing as much as 2,400 pounds. Various European armies used Shires as warhorses, covering them with armor. They were sometimes referred to as living tanks. Some consider Shires slower moving than other draft horse breeds. The breed has not been popular for farmwork.

Suffolk. Country of origin: England. Suffolks have a good disposition, making them easy to control in tandem hitches. They weigh between 1,600 and 2,000 pounds. Some consider them a bit too small for heavy farmwork.[1]

HORSE TERMS

A stallion on display at the Jackson County Fair in central Wisconsin, date unknown
(WHI IMAGE ID 56448)

The world of horses and their equipment has its own vernacular. Of course, horse owners and those who grew up driving horses know "horse language" as well as they know their own.

Carriage horse: A relatively light horse (900 to 1,200 pounds) used for pulling buggies and carriages

Colt: A male up to four years of age

Dam: Mother of a foal

Draft horse: A large workhorse (weighing as much as 2,500 pounds) capable of pulling heavy loads

Filly: A female up to four years of age

Foal: A horse of either sex up to six months old

Gelding: A castrated or neutered male horse

Hand: Equals four inches; used to measure the height of a horse, from the ground to the top of its withers (the shoulder, between the neck and the back)

Mare: An adult female horse

Mustang: Hardy wild horse that descended from Arabian horses brought to North America by the Spanish; brought to the Midwest by horse dealers and sold to farmers to be used as workhorses

Purebred: A horse with ancestors of the same breed

Racehorse: Usually a horse bred to race

Saddle horse: A lightweight horse (might weigh 1,000 pounds) used only for riding

Sire: Father of a foal

Stallion: An adult male horse; also called a stud horse

Yearling: A horse of either sex between one and two years of age

Care and Feeding

During the time when horses were our primary sources for power and transportation, much was written about their care and feeding. Advice for horse care ranged from how to talk to horses to what kinds of stalls to provide them. "A low kind voice and a firm hand will soon inspire his [the horse's] confidence, and then you are reasonably sure of his prompt obedience in most cases of emergency. Never lose your temper when handling a colt. If you do the injury to his manners may be irreparable. Whenever you feel tempted to speak irritably to a horse, just stop and ask yourself how you would relish being spoken to in the same tone. Horses do not understand all words as clearly as men do, but detect an irritating tone of voice even more readily."[2]

Some of the advice was quite curious, at least by today's standards. For instance, a writer for *Farm Journal* magazine wrote in 1858, "Every farmer who keeps horses should have a patch of carrots. They cost less than oats per bushel, and if one bushel of carrots be fed with two bushels of oats, they will do the horse much more good than if three bushels of oats were fed raw. Raise some this year and try them."[3]

NOTES FROM
The Horse Barn

When meeting a horse for the first time: The wrong way is to walk right up to the horse and pat it on the head. The correct way is to speak the horse's name, approach it slowly from the side, and stand a few paces away so the horse can look at you. Then walk up, with hands at your sides, close enough so the horse can smell you. After a few seconds, raise your hand and stroke the animal's neck, while you continue to speak quietly.[4]

Feed

Timothy hay and oats have long been popular feeds for draft horses. Farmers prized timothy for their horses because it was easy to grow, generally free of mold and dust, not likely to spoil when stored, and relished by horses. It was so common at one time that it became widely known as horse hay.

Farmers who began feeding legumes, such as clover and alfalfa, to their horses quickly saw problems. Legumes are more nutritious than timothy hay, and thus horses need to eat less. Indeed, some horses will eat themselves sick when they have easy access to legume hay. What's more, legumes, especially clover, are prone to developing molds when curing, which can create problems for horses. Today, oats are the grain of choice for horses. Although corn can be used, it should be fed as ear corn or shelled corn, not ground.

Good pasture is essential for draft horses, lowering feed bills and human labor as the horse gathers its own feed and providing the animal exercise while grazing. Pastures that offer a mixture of grass, clovers, and alfalfa serve horses best.

HORSES AND THE UNIVERSITY OF WISCONSIN

The University of Wisconsin–Madison made a significant contribution to the study and practice of agriculture with its research and teaching on the care and management of draft horses, especially in the area of feeds and feeding. In 1898 Dean William A. Henry of the College of Agriculture wrote *Feeds and Feeding*, which became the standard textbook on this topic across the country. The book addressed the nutrition needs of all farm animals and included several chapters devoted to horses.

Starting in 1880 and continuing to 1933, the university helped sponsor farmers' institutes—an organized way for farmers to learn from each other and from university experts. The institutes, usually daylong seminars, were conducted in community rooms, the back rooms of taverns, and assorted other gathering places, often during the winter months. Some instructors came from the university; others were farmers from Wisconsin and outside the state who knew about specialized topics such as horses, feeding dairy cattle, or growing alfalfa hay. From their very beginning the institutes proved extremely popular. In 1914 125 institutes were held throughout the state with a total attendance of 114,000. In 1931, during the depths of the Great Depression, 855 Wisconsin communities hosted farmers' institutes with a total attendance of 156,632. The Wisconsin legislature provided funding for the institutes, making them free to attendees.[1]

In 1883 the Wisconsin legislature passed legislation creating an Agricultural Experiment Station on the University of Wisconsin–Madison campus.

With this new source of funds, the university's agricultural research expanded considerably. In 1889 the state legislature created the University of Wisconsin College of Agriculture to provide formal education and grant degrees in agriculture and to conduct research through the Agricultural Experiment Station.[2]

In 1899 the College of Agriculture completed a new horse barn on campus. This magnificent, multi-storied building was designed to house beef cattle in the basement, horses on the second floor (reached by a ramp), vehicles and machinery on the first floor, and hay on the third. The 1899 horse barn was likely a remodeling of a much earlier barn constructed on the same site around 1868, around the time the university hired W. W. Daniels, its first professor of agriculture.[3]

Beginning in 1903 the University of Wisconsin held an annual horse show and auction on the Madison campus. The event, at which the state's farmers could see the best horses in the various breeds and purchase top-rated animals at auction, was a major event on farmers' calendars for many years.

By 1905 the annual horse show and auction had outgrown the university's small dairy barn pavilion. William Henry informed University of Wisconsin president Charles Van Hise that the college needed a new pavilion. A committee (among its members were Frederick Pabst Jr. and several other prominent horse breeders) urged Governor Robert La Follette to recommend the legislature appropriate $80,000 for a new pavilion. The funding was approved, and soon construction was authorized.

(continued on next page)

HORSES AND THE UNIVERSITY OF WISCONSIN

(continued from page 27)

During the planning stage, the university's horse foreman (lead horse caretaker), Joe Delwiche, convinced the planners that their projected arena was too small. As the story goes, Delwiche hitched one of the "fastest stepping light horses to a gig and careened around the too small oval that was laid out for the arena." The result: not merely a larger oval of an arena but a larger building all around.[4]

The University of Wisconsin Stock Pavilion was completed in 1909. The building is two stories high, 115 feet wide by 212 feet long. The first floor features a 66-foot by 164-foot oval area with fixed seating for 2,000 people, expandable to 3,500. The basement once included forty horse stalls. At the time of its completion and until the University of Wisconsin Field House was built in 1930, the stock pavilion was the largest gathering place in Madison. And, unexpectedly, it had excellent acoustics. It became a popular venue for speakers (including Theodore Roosevelt and Harry Truman), bands such as the U.S. Navy Band, and even noted symphony orchestras, including the London Symphony.[5]

Built for horse shows and sales, the stock pavilion has taken on many and varied roles—all conducted in a place with a sawdust-covered floor. And since sometime in the 1940s, university students, no matter what their major, have visited the stock pavilion as one step in their long and tortuous registration process (I was one of those students). No doubt few of them are aware of the university's legacy in teaching farmers about the care and feeding of horses.

Farmers gather at the University of Wisconsin–Madison for a horse show, circa 1905. A major attraction was Pabst Brewing Company's six-horse hitch. (PHOTO FROM THE AUTHOR'S COLLECTION)

NOTES

1. Jerry Apps, *The People Came First: A History of Wisconsin Cooperative Extension* (Madison, WI: University of Wisconsin Extension, 2002), 17–18, 30, 37, 58.

2. Ibid., 18–20.

3. UW–Madison Digital Collections, http://content.library.wisc.edu/cdm4/browse.php?&CISCOSTART=1.

4. Gustav Bohstedt, *Early History of Animal Husbandry and Related Departments* (Madison, WI: Meat and Animal Science Dept., 1973), 35.

5. UW–Madison Digital Collections, http://content.library.wisc.edu/cdm4/browse.php?&CISCOSTART=1.

The amount of feed a working horse requires depends on its weight and other factors. Some horses are "easy keepers," able to maintain their weight and energy with less feed than the "hard keepers" need. Generally, horses working seven to eight hours a day at hard work need about one pound of grain and one pound of hay per one hundred pounds of weight. Of course, a horse needs plenty of good water, too; a working horse may drink ten to twelve gallons of water per day.[5]

Stables

Horse barns dotted Wisconsin's landscape well before dairy barns did. In the 1850s to 1870s, when Wisconsin was primarily a wheat-growing state, most farmers owned only a few cows that foraged for feed and huddled around straw stacks to keep warm in winter. But farmers knew how important their horses were to the success of the farm, and for the most part they treated their horses very well. The farming manuals and magazines of the time included many recommendations about horse barns. Writers agreed that a horse stable must have proper light and ventilation and should provide "comfort and security of the horses and convenience of attendants."[6] Throughout Wisconsin farm country, horse stables ranged from a corner in a barn otherwise used for dairy cows to a large building that housed only horses. A horse's stall should be at least four feet wide, preferably five feet—wide enough so the horse can lie down. If the stall is too narrow, not only is it uncomfortable for the horse, but it allows the horse to squeeze a person against the side of the stall. Wooden planks are better than concrete for the floor of a stall, as concrete floors will excessively wear a horse's hoofs.

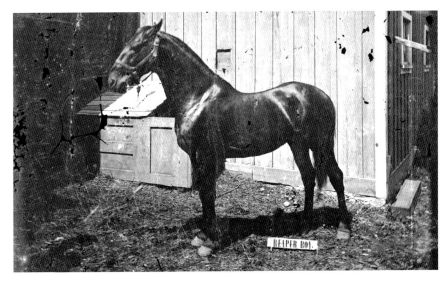

During the 1870s Norwegian immigrant Andreas Larsen Dahl took many photographs of Wisconsin families and their homes, farms, and most cherished possessions, including this one of Reaper Boy at his stable in Prairie du Sac, circa 1877. (WHI IMAGE ID 27257)

Breaking and Training

Books of the early 1900s contained considerable advice about breaking and training horses. For example, in his work *The People's Home Stock Book*, published in 1910, W. C. Fair suggested that

> *the most successful horse breakers and trainers are level-headed, good natured and thoughtful men and they make a study of every colt or horse that comes under their care for instruction. They believe in subduing the animal by kindness rather than by force; they also know that it is important to teach certain lessons first, also to get on good terms with the animal.*

Fair went on to provide very specific instructions for halter breaking a colt:

> *In order that the work may be accomplished easily, a colt should be halter broke when it is a few days old, or not allowed to go longer than two or three weeks. Put a halter on the colt and lead the mare and the colt with her. Lead the colt short distances to and from the mare and also in a circle within her view. Teach him the word to stop and start, lift up his feet, open his mouth, avoid frightening him, don't use the whip as it is unnecessary.*
>
> > *Handle him often enough so that he will not forget his lessons or acquaintance with you. When halter breaking him teach him to stand tied and be sure to use a halter that he cannot break, for if he learns the habit of breaking loose he soon becomes a halter puller. . . . The older and stronger a colt is when you attempt to halter break him, the more force must be used; besides, it takes more time and he is more likely to get hurt.[7]*

Fair firmly believed in treating horses humanely and respecting their basic intelligence.

> *When we consider what remarkable memories horses possess and what respect they have for man if treated kindly by him, we should not feel discouraged at the simple task of teaching horses to stand without hitching, stop and start when they are told, quicken and slow their gait at the word, go to the right or left when asked and to back when told, without the use of reins. . . . An animal should be talked to, but not foolishly. Say to them what you want them to do, show them how, then it is only a question of a sufficient number of lessons when they will do what they are told.[8]*

NOTES FROM

The Horse Barn

The life expectancy of a horse is twenty to thirty years.

Howard Peck recalls the time when some untrained colts arrived on his family's farm in Chippewa County. In 1934 a sleeping sickness epidemic killed the Pecks' horses. With no money to purchase new horses, Peck's father traded some cows for a pair of colts. The young horses, each weighing about seven hundred pounds, had been shipped to Wisconsin by a horse trader who had gotten them from the West. Howard, fifteen at the time, and his brothers Richard, seventeen, and Leonard, thirteen, got involved in the colts' training. Peck remembers, "They came to us wild. By playing with them, my brothers and I tamed them so they seemed quite gentle. . . . Together, the three of us felt capable of doing anything with these horses."

One summer day the boys decided to hitch the colts as a team—though they realized their father, who was an experienced horseman, would not have approved. Howard stood at the head of one colt and Leonard stood at the head of the other, while Richard hooked the harness tugs to the doubletree (see page 40) they planned to fasten to a stoneboat some distance away.

Richard held the lines. Before the team of colts had taken three steps, they felt the doubletree behind them and took off at full speed. Richard fell down, sliding on his belly across the manure-strewn barnyard as he held tight to the harness lines. He was dragged for about a hundred yards before he let go. The colts galloped through the open barnyard

CIRCUS WORLD HORSE BARN

An interesting old horse barn stands at Circus World Museum in Baraboo, Wisconsin, the site for many years of the Ringling Brothers Circus winter quarters. Built in 1904, the barn included stalls for one hundred Percheron horses, plus an area at one end where a blacksmith could work. The building housed Ringling horses every winter until the circus left Baraboo in the fall of 1918. After the Ringlings left, the barn stood empty until 1933, when local judge Adolph Andro and businessman Fred Effinger purchased the barn and other winter quarters buildings. The new owners rented the buildings to local businesses and began selling them in 1939; the Schwarz Farm Equipment Company bought the horse barn. In 1959 Circus World Museum opened on the Ringling Brothers winter quarters site, having acquired several of the original buildings. Money for the purchase came from a statewide fund-raising drive plus $10,000 from the Baraboo City Council. Today, visitors to the museum can visit the barn, see where the horses stood, and think about what it must have been like when one hundred circus horses were housed there.[1]

NOTES

1. Jerry Apps, *Ringlingville USA* (Madison: Wisconsin Historical Society Press, 2005), 115.

Training horses requires patience and skill. Here a man trains a horse to become accustomed to a halter and rope, Black River Falls, Wisconsin, date unknown.
(WHI IMAGE ID 43713)

gate and up the road for a mile or so, scattering harness parts as they ran. The brothers finally rounded up the colts and brought them home. Peck has never forgotten the incident. "My brothers and I had learned not to hitch two untrained colts as a team."[9]

Walter Bjoraker, who grew up on a farm near Owatonna, Minnesota, recalls this story about breaking a young horse his father had purchased:

> The first time any young horse is hitched to a wagon to learn basic commands can be an exciting time. My father usually bought an experienced horse when replacements were needed, but not this time. Chub was a magnificent two-year-old Percheron and large for his age. He had an arched neck and lots of energy. He had been raised from the mare, Dolly. He was to be hitched for the first time with his mother as a teammate.
>
> Dad was usually uneasy around spirited horses, having spent his youth on a small farm in Norway, giving him little experience with horses. This morning, Dad gave sharp commands in Norwegian to two of my older brothers, telling them to hold tightly the ropes tied to Chub's halter. Dad climbed aboard the wagon, and I could see from the expression on his face he expected some excitement as he gripped the reins, giving the command, "Giddy-up."
>
> After several well-executed turns in the farmyard, Dad shouted, "Whoa." Both stopped as a well-trained team should. Instantly, Dad sensed Chub was not a stranger to the harness, and he guessed why. He struggled between anger at my brothers and laughter, and laughter won out.

My brothers admitted whenever Dad went to town, they had ridden Chub bareback in the pasture as well has harnessed and hitched him to the buggy. In fact, years later, as my brothers became adults, they revealed that one of them had ridden Chub on an occasion when he became out of control, running among the trees in the pasture. A low-hanging branch knocked one of my brothers to the ground. Luckily, the event resulted only in bruises, so they didn't have to tell Ma and Pa and therefore did not get chastised for their mischievous behavior.[10]

Diseases and Illnesses

Because there were so many horses during the late 1800s and into the early 1900s, dealing with their ailments and injuries became a big business. Lameness was a common ailment, its cause often obscure. Farm papers ran ads proclaiming, "How to cure that lame horse free. . . . We want to show you that there isn't any affliction that causes lameness in horses that can't be cured no matter how longstanding. . . . Mack's Spavin Remedy is guaranteed to relieve the very worst case of lameness . . . will not leave a mark or blemish of any kind. If the remedy fails every cent that you paid out will be returned to you."[11]

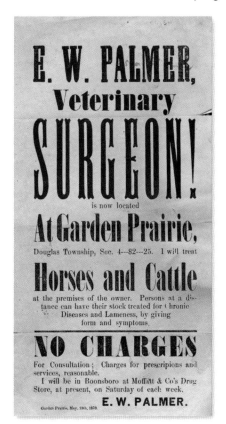

Veterinarian E. W. Palmer of Garden Prairie, Iowa, issued this broadside in 1870 advertising his large-animal services. (WHI IMAGE ID 42402)

Dr. J. Robert Curtis of Portage, Wisconsin, graduated from the veterinary school at Ohio State University in 1938. Curtis remembers traveling as a boy with his veterinary father, Charles R. Curtis, who in 1910 was the first graduate veterinarian in Portage. (For many years so-called horse doctors with practical knowledge and no formal training treated horses in many farm and rural communities.)

Dr. Curtis recalls the early 1930s, the years of drought and sandstorms: "Up in Adams County the sand was blowing all over and there was nothing but little weeds trying to come up. There was no pasture, no hay. I can remember going with my father and posting [doing a postmortem] on horses that had died. Their stomachs were full of sand. The horses, trying to nibble on the sparse grass and weeds, also got a mouth of sand. It was called sand colic and was fairly common at the time."[12]

According to Curtis, the most common cause of lameness was stepping on a nail or piece of wire. He describes other common ailments:

Taking care of horses' teeth was a regular task. Horse teeth continue to grow, different from humans. Thus, "floating" [smoothing a horse's teeth with a file] was a common task. Sometimes a horse's tooth had

HORSE COLORS

You might think horses are either black, white, brown, or tan. But horse color is considerably more complicated, ranging from gray to bay, from sorrel to roan, from palomino to chestnut.

Bay: Reddish brown, ranging from light to dark, with black legs from hoof to knee; black tail and mane

Black: Entirely black, except for some white on the face

Blond sorrel: Reddish brown with blond mane and tail

Buckskin: Deep cream to sand color; black mane and tail

Roan: Tan with darker mane and tail

Sorrel or chestnut: Reddish brown with tan or brown mane and tail

Dapple gray: Small white marks (dapples) covering the entire gray body

Gray: Light gray, not white; black skin around nose and between hind legs

Palomino: Tan with lighter mane and tail

White: Pure white horses are extremely rare— most that are thought to be white are actually gray. There also are albino horses.

to be pulled. Often teeth must be cut. That was probably one of the most common things we did. Another common problem was internal parasites, common bots [the bot fly larvae attach to the stomach and small intestine] that could rupture a horse's stomach and cause death. We used a special drug, carbon disulfide, to treat infected animals.

Curtis recounts that often farmers would make arrangements to have the veterinarian visit several of them on one trip. "The farmers knew to withhold the feed for their horses before the veterinarian arrived. Dad—and later I—would make the rounds treating the horses in the neighborhood and at the same time fix the horses' teeth. Dad was one of the first ones in the area to do that sort of thing."[13]

Sleeping sickness (equine encephalomyelitis) devastated the horse population in the late 1930s. Mosquitoes transmitted the virus that caused the disease, which also affected people and birds. The virus attacked a horse's central nervous system; one day a horse would appear normal, and the next day it would be staggering. Depending on the virus strain, mortality rates would be as high as 90 percent. Today vaccination is used to prevent the disease.

Curtis remembers, "In 1938, when I started practice with my father, sleeping sickness had reached its peak in the Midwest. That ended the use of horses on many farms, because so many horses died. . . . By 1940 a vaccine had been developed, and we started to vaccinate horses for the disease."[14]

Breeding

Many farmers owned a brood mare or two, which they bred to a neighbor's stallion or to one owned by a breeder with a traveling stallion who made the rounds of farm communities. Most farmers did not own stallions, which could be a nuisance, even dangerous, especially when the mares came in season. The occasional farmer owned a stallion or two that he sent around to farmers who wanted their mares bred. When a stallion sired outstanding foals, the word spread rapidly and the demand for the stallion increased.

Jim Erb, who grew up in farm country in Illinois, remembers that his grandfather, John, kept stallions, usually Percherons, at his 320-acre dairy and grain farm near Naperville. John Erb had a full time hired man who took one of the stallions from farm to farm to breed mares. The hired man tied the stallion behind a buggy and bred mares all over northern Illinois. The breeding fee was twenty dollars. One year John Erb had two stallions making the rounds. The men Erb hired for this task were down on their luck fellows from the county home; they got their meals from the farm owners and sometimes would stay overnight at a farm.[15]

Horse breeding was a profitable undertaking for some farmers. Here a man shows off a breeding stallion, perhaps a Clydesdale or Shire, date unknown.

(WHI IMAGE ID 53811)

Harness and Equipment

As farmers replaced oxen with horses, the demand for leather harnesses increased dramatically, and by the mid-1800s harness making was a prominent business. Many of the harness-making shops were tiny, with but one or two workers. In these shops skilled craftspeople working with tanned hides made harnesses, horse collars, halters, bridles, and sometimes even the fancy decorations for horse-drawn buggies. Most harness makers also did steady business repairing and reconditioning harnesses. In 1870 the United States census reported 7,607 harness makers in the country, and harness and saddle making ranked thirty-fourth among all professions in the number of people employed.[17]

One of the most famous harness makers in Wisconsin and Iowa was August Ringling, father of the Ringling brothers. German-born August Ringling arrived in Milwaukee in 1848 and worked there as a harness maker; he later owned harness shops in McGregor, Iowa, and Baraboo, Wisconsin. His seven sons all worked in their father's harness shop before they went on to organize and operate the world-famous Ringling Brothers Circus.[18]

By 1900 the craft of harness making began to disappear as cheaper factory-made harnesses became widely available. The 1908 Sears, Roebuck and Co. catalog offered draft horse harnesses for $20.99: "Lines one inch wide, 20 feet long, good heavy, well selected line leather, well made. Wood hames iron bound, square staple, Concord clip attachment for hame tug. . . . Weight of harness, boxed for shipment about 70 pounds."[19]

Lyle Goman operated a one-man harness shop in my hometown of Wild Rose, Wisconsin, when I was growing up. Goman also made halters for cattle and for horses in addition to working as a shoemaker. But by the 1930s and 1940s, shops such as Goman's had moved from harness making to harness repair. Goman closed his shop sometime in the late 1950s.

What I remember most about Goman's little shop are the smells that engulfed me as I entered: leather, leather dye, and cabbage cooking. Lyle and his wife lived in back of the shop, and it seems they were quite fond of cabbage—or perhaps they couldn't afford much else. Goman was severely disabled. He used a crutch to get around his shop, but he always had a smile on his face, and he seemed to enjoy the kids who came in with their broken horse bridles or shoes with soles that needed replacing.

Horse harnesses, for many years made of leather, with brass and other metal for rings and chains, have a unique vocabulary for their various parts:

Belly band: A piece of leather that fits around the middle of the horse like a belt and buckles under the animal's belly.

Bit: A strip of metal attached to a bridle that fits in a horse's mouth. The bits come in various shapes and sizes, and the style used depends on how easy or difficult it is to control a particular horse.

Breeching or britchin: A heavy piece of leather at the back end of the harness that fits around the horse's rump and assists the horse when backing an implement.

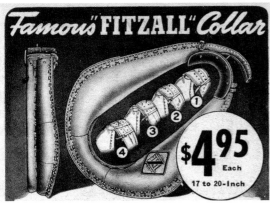

You Save by Buying Replacement Hames at Sears

(SEARS, ROEBUCK CATALOG, 1940)

Bridle: A leather device that fits over a horse's head and includes a metal bit. The leather lines used to steer the team are attached to the horse's bridle and bit.

Collar: A piece of leather stuffed with straw and formed so it fastens around a horse's neck. Collars come in various sizes, based on the size of the horse's neck. A properly fitting collar is key to a happy, good-pulling horse, as all of the weight to be pulled is applied to the collar. Collars have hame grooves where the harness hames fit.

Collar pad: A heavy piece of cloth that fits between the horse's neck and the leather collar.

Halter: A leather device that fits over a horse's head and is used for tying or leading the horse. A halter does not include a bit.

Hames: Two wooden (occasionally metal) strips that buckle to each side of the horse collar. The tugs and other major leather components of the harness are fastened to the hames. Hames often have decorative brass or other metal balls at the top.

Hip-drop assembly: Comprises the hip straps, which hold the breeching, and a hook to fasten the tug chains.

Reins (lines): Long pieces of leather snapped to the horse's bridle and used to control the horse. Pulling on the left line steers the horse to the left; pulling on the right line steers to the right. Pulling back on the reins and commanding "back" tells the team to back up.

Tugs: Thick leather straps attached to the hames on each side of the horse's collar. A short length of chain is attached to the end of each tug. The chain is used to hitch the horse to a singletree (see page 40).

Yoke strap: Found on the bottom of the horse collar and used to attach the neck yoke (see page 40).

HOW TO HARNESS A HORSE

I'd forgotten how difficult harnessing a horse can be. After all, I hadn't harnessed one since I was sixteen or seventeen years old. So recently I asked Laverne Forest, who with his wife, Betty, owns and operates Eplegaarden Orchard in Fitchburg, Wisconsin, if he could spare some time to show me how he harnesses his team of Belgians.

The Forests use Buck and Doll for hayrides and orchard tours, so most of the time the horses laze their days away on the sloping hills of a lush pasture. They are blond sorrels, which means they are reddish brown with blond manes and tails, and both are seventeen years old. Together the team weighs nearly two tons; Buck weighs about a ton, and Doll is a couple hundred pounds lighter. The weight of the team is a solid reminder to the driver that he or she doesn't want either one of them to plant a hoof on his or her foot. That part of harnessing a horse I haven't forgotten.

I arrived at Eplegaarden on a warm spring day for my harnessing refresher. As he gathered the equipment, Laverne told me, "Doll is the left horse. Buck is the right horse. That's how they are hitched. And that's how I store their harnesses in the barn."

"You start by letting the horse know you are there," Laverne continued. "A few words spoken softly are sufficient," he pointed out. Otherwise, you might startle the horse, and it might kick you. "You always work from the left side of the horse," Laverne said. **❶**

First Laverne put the collar over Doll's head, fastening the leather strap at the top of the collar and making sure the collar was not too tight on the horse's neck. He checked the tightness by putting his hand between the collar and the horse's neck at the bottom of the collar. **❷**

"The horse really pushes the load rather than pulling it," Laverne said. "That's why it's so important the collar fits right."

After putting on the collar, Laverne gathered up the harness—they can cost as little as three hundred dollars and more than one thousand dollars for those heavily decorated with silver—and slid the hames into the slots on the collar. He placed the remainder of the harness on Doll's back and fastened the hames to the collar with the top and bottom hame straps. **❸** He pulled the bottom strap as tight as possible so the hames were one with the collar. **❹** All the while Laverne worked, he was quietly talking to the team.

Next he straightened out the breaching over Doll's rump and freed her tail. The breaching is

HOW TO HARNESS A HORSE

especially important when the team is backing an implement, as the horses push against this piece of leather to give them purchase. Laverne aligned the back strap to which the belly band was attached. Then he buckled the belly band, which ran under the horse, making sure the snap's spring clip was away from the horse's skin to prevent irritation.❺ Next he snapped the reins onto the hames. Laverne checked to make sure all the leather pieces of the harness lay flat with no twists, which would irritate the horse.

With Doll harnessed, he proceeded to harness Buck in the same way. When both were harnessed, he put a bridle on Doll, first working the bit into her mouth and then pulling the remainder of the bridle over her head. He did the same with Buck. A bit does not hurt the horse's mouth, but if a horse refuses a command, a gentle tug on the reins is transferred to the horse's mouth, reminding the animal to pay attention.❻

Laverne then straightened the lines and snapped the left line to the left ring on Doll's bit and the right line to the right ring of Buck's bit. The horses were ready for hitching to a wagon. Laverne fastened each horse's collar to the neck yoke with neck yoke straps, which were attached to the bottom of each horse collar. He fastened the neck yoke to the front of the implement's tongue. Last, Laverne hooked the tug chains to the singletrees, which together are part of a doubletree.❼ ❽

Harnessing and hitching a team takes time, patience, and a good understanding of one's horses. It can be hard work. The harnesses are heavy, and draft horses are tall. An improperly harnessed horse will be uncomfortable and less productive and even can develop harness sores. Some horses do not like to be harnessed (I suspect they may simply not enjoy working) and may try to crowd the horseperson against the stall while being harnessed, especially if the person is a child. I have less-than-fond memories of the experience.

SEARS LEADER Our 4-Star Feature Harness

Farmers relied on the Sears, Roebuck catalog for many years as a source of harnesses and other equipment. In its 1940 catalog, Sears featured the Leader harness for $48.90, "equal to the toughest jobs to which you'll ever put your teams." (SEARS, ROEBUCK CATALOG, 1940)

With the horse in harness, another set of equipment with unique names is necessary to hitch the horse to the wagon, plow, or whatever requires pulling:

Buggy shafts: Two long pieces of wood between which a horse is hitched to a vehicle, such as a buggy or a cart.

Doubletree: A swinging crossbar (often made of wood) to which smaller bars (singletrees) are attached. It is used when two horses are hitched side by side to pull a wagon or other farm implement.

Neck yoke: A bar (usually wood but sometimes metal) that is fastened to a horse-drawn implement's tongue. When a team is hitched to the implement, the neck yoke is suspended from the collars of the harnesses.

Singletree: A single crossbar (usually wood) to which the tugs of a horse harness are fastened. The center of the singletree is attached to a doubletree. A singletree is also known as a whiffletree or whippletree.

Tongue: A pole attached to the front axle of a horse-drawn implement that is pulled by a team of horses.

Horseshoeing and Blacksmiths

No one seems to know who invented the first horseshoe, but evidence suggests early Asian horsepeople used leather materials on their horse's hooves to protect them. During the first century AD the Romans began using a type of metal horseshoe, and nailed-on iron horseshoes became popular during the time of the Crusades (1096–1270). In 1835 Henry Burden of Troy, New York, obtained the first patent for a horseshoe-manufacturing machine.[20]

NOTES FROM

The Horse Barn

One of the most important factors in a horse's health is hoof maintenance. Improper hoof care can cause injury and disease.

But while horseshoeing was becoming more common—especially for horses that walked on hard surfaces such as cobbled city streets and paved roads and for some working horses, such as those in the logging industry and the circus—most farmers did not shoe their horses, allowing them to go "barefoot." A horse's hoof is continually growing, but the hoof wears away rapidly if the horse walks on hard surfaces. Except for trips to haul produce to town or to transport the farmer somewhere or another, farm horses walked on relatively soft ground and didn't require shoes.

Horseshoeing evolved into a task of the blacksmith, who knew how to work with metal and who had the forge, anvil, and other necessary equipment. Most blacksmiths who shod horses also repaired broken farm machinery, fashioned plow points, and made door latches and butcher knives—truly a jack-of-all-trades. Many blacksmiths even made their own horseshoe nails from a straight bar of steel they heated on their forge and then cut and shaped on their anvil. Almost every village of any size had its blacksmith, so farmers and others who needed horses shod did not have far to travel for their services.

G. F. Koehler, longtime blacksmith in Merrill, Wisconsin, arrived there in 1859. A Merrill newspaper reported some of his memories in 1921:

> *The busiest season of the year was autumn and the hardest horses to shoe were the young unbroken horses. But the hardest of all animals to shoe was the mule as he, without any warning, sends out his back heels with unusual force.*
>
> *The average number of horses shod in a day was from five to six. In the summer, generally only the front feet require shoeing while in the winter the shoeing is all around.*
>
> *With an average of eight nails to a shoe, Mr. Koehler drove close to 2,000,000 nails into horses' hoofs in his lifetime, counting those which failed to gain a hold and which had to be replaced.*
>
> *The average price of fitting a horse with shoes in Mr. Koehler's day was about seventy-five cents where the old shoes were replaced and $1.50 where new shoes were used. About half of Koehler's income came from horseshoeing.*[21]

Workers at the C. Deising
horseshoe shop, Milwaukee,
early 1900s
(WHI IMAGE ID 57302)

Much of the work once done by blacksmiths, including repairing farm machinery, was eventually taken over by the machinery dealers. Horseshoeing, too, became a specialty, and the person who did the work became known as a farrier. (At one time the word *farrier* referred to a horse doctor, but the meaning has changed over the years.) According to the *Oxford English Dictionary*, the Latin root of the word *farrier* is *ferrarius*, referring to iron.

But farmers are a self-sufficient lot, and some preferred to do their own horseshoeing. Sears, Roebuck and Co. sold horseshoes, steel bars for nails, and horseshoeing equipment for many years. In the company's 1940 catalog, horseshoes sold for from 24 cents to 79 cents each. A complete horseshoeing outfit consisting of buffer, knife, pritchel (hoof pick), hammer, rasp, and cutting nippers cost $3.95. An extra-large-size blacksmith's leather apron was available for $2.49.[22]

HORSES AND PEOPLE

By 1919 the number of draft horses in the United States reached a pinnacle of twenty-six million.[1] Just as automobiles are integral to the lives of nearly everyone today, horses were vital in the nineteenth and early twentieth centuries. It didn't matter if you lived on a farm, in a small town, or in the city, horses provided the means of getting from here to there. When railroads arrived, by the mid-1800s, they began providing the majority of the long-distance transportation. But much other getting around involved horses. Draft horses pulled the delivery wagons hauling lumber, beer, and other heavy commodities. They toted the wagons that picked up people at the train depots and transported them to the hotels. And before trains, draft horses pulled the stagecoaches that tied villages and cities together.

The Place for Wagons

For farm people, the same wagon that hauled corn and hay from the field was the one they drove to the nearest village for supplies. The earliest of these farm wagons were made by local blacksmiths and wagon makers and truly were works of art. Local craftspeople built the high wagon wheels with wooden spokes, framed by a round metal rim. The wagon's wooden box usually included a spring seat toward the front, where the driver and a passenger could sit.

Wagon making was big business from the mid-1800s to the early 1900s, with dozens of small and large manufacturers located around the country. John Deere's wagon works in Moline, Illinois, built in 1854, grew to a half million square feet of floor space and a capacity for building thirty thousand wagons a year by 1937—the same year the company proclaimed itself the largest wagon factory in the world.[2]

The H. and C. Studebaker blacksmith shop opened in South Bend, Indiana, in 1852, and in time Studebaker became a major manufacturer of high-wheeled farm wagons, eventually calling itself—just like John Deere—the largest wagon maker in the world. In a 1908 wagon ad the company boasted, "Do you wonder that it lasts? Do you

wonder that it is the wagon with a reputation behind it? You cannot afford to buy a 'cheap' wagon, when you can get the best for so little. It is poor economy to be constantly paying out money for repair bills. Get a Studebaker and save money."[3] (The company began making electric automobiles in 1902 and gasoline-powered cars in 1904. It made automobiles until 1966.[4])

Not to be outdone by John Deere and Studebaker, the Kentucky Wagon Company of Louisville, Kentucky, advertised in 1911, "Save $10 to $30. Largest wagon factory in the world now sells direct to farmers at low factory prices—freight prepaid. Get the most famous, most perfect wagons made—an 'Old Hickory' or a 'Tennessee.'"[5]

Wisconsin was home to many carriage and wagon manufacturers. An 1850 directory listed seventy-four wagon-making firms in the state.[6] The Bain Wagon Works of Kenosha began operations in 1870 and became one of the largest; by 1879 the company was making ten thousand wagons a year, employed three hundred people, and occupied four city blocks.[7]

The Stoughton Wagon Company of Stoughton began in 1865 as the T. G. Mandt Works. It advertised, "The Stoughton Wagon, the best is the cheapest. Most complete wagon in the market."[8]

One-Horse Cast Skein Wagon with Wood Hub Wheels.

Sears, Roebuck offered an array of farm wagons. The company's 1908 catalog offered this wooden-wheeled model.
(SEARS, ROEBUCK CATALOG, 1908)

By 1940 Sears offered a steel-wheeled wagon, along with wagon boxes.
(SEARS, ROEBUCK CATALOG, 1940)

By the late 1800s steel-wheeled farm wagons began replacing the high-wheeled wagons for general farm duty. These new wagons' steel wheels were sturdier and built closer to the ground so the wagon could be loaded more easily. Capitalizing on the advancement, the Electric Wheel Company of Quincy, Illinois, proclaimed in its ads: "You will live longer if you will save all the vast amount of energy and nervous force you expend yearly loading the old fashioned high wheel wagons."[9]

For several decades, as long as farmers drove teams to pull their wagons and horses provided the main power source on farms, steel-wheeled wagons remained popular, essentially replacing all or nearly all of the wooden-spoked, high-wheeled wagons. Later, with the coming of tractors, rubber-tired wagons would replace those with steel wheels.

Horse Trading

Nearly every farmer was a horse trader at one time or another. A horse died and had to be replaced, farming operations expanded and a new team became necessary, or an old pair of horses couldn't quite do the required work anymore. The term *horse trader* referred to anyone who dealt in horses, whether actual trades or outright purchases. Newspapers and farm magazines carried ads for horses of almost every age and breed. Nearly every village had its local horse dealer who traded horses full time. Today we'd compare these local horse traders to used-car salespeople; unfortunately, their reputations were quite similar, perhaps even worse. A common description of the horse dealer was, "He goes to church on Sunday, but watch out for him on Monday."

Many of these often-unscrupulous dealers maintained small stockyards in villages across the Midwest. They would constantly buy and sell horses, obtaining their stock from farm auctions and from farmers who wanted to trade for one reason or another. Some horse traders even brought in mustangs from the West, in railroad stock cars, and

NOTES FROM

The Horse Barn

Horses are social animals and feel most secure when they are with other horses.

sold them to area farmers. Of course, many of these mustangs were wild horses who had never seen a harness or saddle. They became quite a challenge to the farmer who was accustomed to the more docile Percheron or Belgian draft horses. But the mustangs were smaller and lighter than the typical draft horse, which made them attractive for farmers who wanted them to pull a carriage or a one-horse walking cultivator.

Dr. J. Robert Curtis, longtime veterinarian in Portage, Wisconsin, recalled dealers shipping western horses into Portage, twenty or thirty to a railroad stock car: "A cowboy would stand in the center; a farmer would pick out a horse he wanted and the cowboy roped it for him and tied the horse to a fence so the farmer could put a halter on the animal. Most farmers would bring their draft horse teams to town. They'd put the western horse between the two horses of the team and drive the new horse home that way. These western horses weren't even halter broke."[10]

Every farmer considered himself a good judge of horse flesh, but horse trading required a healthy dose of "buyer beware." A savvy farmer checked everything about the horse, from observing how it walked and breathed to looking at its teeth (a way to determine its age) to checking its skin for signs of abuse or disease. A good horse buyer always made sure the horse in question had clear eyes. And, of course, the farmer assessed the horse's disposition: did the horse kick at everything that came near, bite you on the arm when you least expected it, rear up and strike you with its front hooves? Once the prospective buyer completed the inspection, buyer and seller haggled over the price, sometimes for hours on end, before striking a deal. The buyer took the horse home, believing he or she had bettered the seller, and of course the seller, especially a professional horse trader, believed the same thing. Usually the horse trader got the better end of the deal, having handled hundreds of horses and seen about every disease, deformity, behavior disorder, or other shortcoming along the way.

W. C. Fair, author of *The People's Home S   k*, a popular 1910 guide, included three "Tricks of Horse   , —ways horse traders tried to cover up disease, blem   d even a horse's disposition. For instance, if the horse   witcher"—meaning it switched its tail a lot—a few hours before the sale the horse trader would hang a four- or five-pound weight to the tail or tie the tail up over the horse's back. These tricks would temporarily paralyze the horse's tail—at least long enough for the sale to take place.[11]

Having sold the Laurel Hill Horse Farm at Fox Lake, and retiring from the active breeding of horses, I am offering some very choice young stallions at exceptionally low prices. Address :

F. C. Warren

VALLEY JUNCTION, WIS.

A horse trader's newspaper ad, 1905 (*WISCONSIN VALLEY SETTLER*, APRIL 15, 1905)

HOW SMART ARE HORSES?

Horses are quite smart, as anyone who has worked around the animals will attest. In their book *Horse Facts*, authors Susan McBane and Helen Douglas-Cooper offer several examples of horses that learned to open stable door latches, remove lids from oat buckets, and remember certain things that happen at a given time each day—feeding time, watering time, and so on. They also pointed out that some horses seem more intelligent than others, sort of like people.[1]

Bob Burull, who grew up near Stoughton, Wisconsin, in the 1940s, remembers a big mixed-breed horse his father owned named Kate. "One early winter day when Dad and I led the horses to the ice-covered water tank, Kate walked up to the tank, took a sniff, snorted, then suddenly reared back on her hind legs like an unruly Arabian and smashed down on the ice with her front hooves, opening up the tank water." Somewhere in her history, Kate had learned how to break ice in order to get a drink of water.[2]

Many horse people agree that horses have good memories. Jerry Kronschnabel, who grew up driving horses in Outagamie County in northeastern Wisconsin, recalls one snowy Sunday afternoon when he hitched his family's draft horse, Queen, to the bobsled and drove off to take a schoolmate on a sleigh ride. The boys and Queen were having a grand time, until Queen slipped on a snow-covered patch of ice and fell. The frightened horse got tangled in the harness and the bobsled shafts, and the children had a difficult time helping her up.

Once Queen was standing, she refused to walk on the road. Jerry drove her home through the fields, a trip of more than five miles that would have been two miles by road. After that day, Queen refused to leave the barn when she detected that there was fresh snow.[3]

Jim Erb recalls this story about his grandfather, John, traveling a few miles by horse and buggy to court his grandmother, Estella Mohler. "He would go to see her at night, after the chores were done. He was usually tired from doing farmwork all day. On the way back home he had to cross a railroad tracks. One night he fell asleep as the horse and buggy were coming home. He woke up to the sound of a train whistle. The horse had stopped by the tracks to wait for the train to pass." Sounds like a smart horse with a memory of trains and train crossings.[4]

NOTES

1. Susan McBane and Helen Douglas-Cooper, *Horse Facts* (New York: Barnes & Noble Books, 1993), 20.

2. Robert Burull, personal correspondence, March 11, 2007.

3. Jerry Kronschnabel, personal correspondence, September 15, 2006.

4. Jim Erb, interview, Lake Mills, WI, September 7, 2006.

NOTES FROM

The Horse Barn

"Price of horses at the Chicago market in February, 1893

Draft horses: 1,500–1,700 pounds, $140–$230

Express horses: 1,450–1,550 pounds, $155–$200

Driving horses: $100–$250 (with some choice actors and very fast road horses considerably higher) These quotations were for sound, well broke horses in good flesh, from five to eight years old."[13]

Fair called another interesting trick "The Stool-Pigeon Swindle": "In all large cities, it is common practice with many disreputable horse dealers to advertise a horse as being the property of Mrs. Blank, who is represented to the customer as a widow. She of course is always dressed in black and sheds tears with ease while in reality she is the 'stool-pigeon' or accomplice of the swindler. Various misrepresentations are made and after the swindle is discovered by the purchaser he is either unable to find the sellers or he finds them to be irresponsible parties from whom no damages can be collected." To avoid this type of swindle, the book's author cautioned, "Beware of 'stool-pigeons' and widows (when buying horses) and have a doubt in your mind when answering advertisements of this kind." Fair also warned his readers about "Dark Trick": "Horse traders frequently desire to dispose of horses that are suffering from moon blindness (periodic ophthalmia). This is an incurable eye defect which is much worse at some times than others. These horses are usually disposed of in the evening or at the times when they show the defect the least." The author's advice, "Never buy a horse in the dark."[12]

Horses played a major role in the circus, both as performers and as work animals. A large circus might own as many as three hundred horses at one time, so it's no surprise that circuses were active horse traders as well. In the early 1910s the Ringling Brothers Circus, based in Baraboo, Wisconsin, owned as many as five hundred horses. The Ringlings' boss hostler (the person responsible for all the horses), Spencer Alexander, was constantly buying and selling horses, especially Percherons. He bought from horse dealers; he bought from farmers; he bought good horses wherever he could find them.

When the circus got to town, farmers came by to get a look at the stock and to try to set up a trade with Alexander. Farmers who traded with Alexander liked to brag that they owned a former circus horse. They also liked to believe they had beaten Alexander in the deal—after all, what did a circus guy know about horses? But Spencer Alexander was one of the best horsemen around. It was a rare day when anyone beat him in a horse deal.

When it was in its heyday, the Ringling Brothers Circus traveled with as many as five hundred horses. Pictured here are Ringling Brothers Circus wagons, horses, and tents with the Chicago skyline in the background, date unknown.
(WHI IMAGE ID 12414)

The Ringling Brothers Circus also bought, from farmers and other sources, scores of what they called broken-down horses, which they slaughtered and used as animal feed for their meat-eating animals, such as lions and tigers.[14]

When Autos Arrived

Automobiles began appearing in major cities by 1900, and their numbers skyrocketed as technology improved. There were 8,000 automobiles registered in the United States in 1900 and 27 million by 1929.[15] Wisconsin had 26,690 registered automobiles by 1912 and 800,000 by 1930, when 84 percent of Wisconsin's farm families owned automobiles.[16]

One of the farm horse's major jobs disappeared as automobiles began providing transportation for the farm family. But while horses no longer hauled milk to the cheese factory, grain to the gristmill, and the family to church, they continued to do the majority of the on-farm work for several more years, until tractors began appearing just before World War II.

And even after automobiles began to supplant them as the family's mode of transport, horses continued to prove themselves a reliable option, often aiding stranded motorists. Especially in winter and spring, country roads often became impassable, and many a trusty team of horses saved the day. Jerry Kronschnabel of Outagamie County in northeastern Wisconsin remembers the time a car got stuck in the mud in front of his family's farm. Jerry's dad took Queen and Belle out to help the driver. He hitched the team to the car, but they would scarcely tighten the tugs. The car was completely strange to them.

Jerry's dad took the horses back to the barn. He returned a few minutes later, now with the team pulling the stoneboat, something they did often. Jerry's dad stretched the chain out over the stoneboat, hooked it to the car, and clucked to the team. Now Queen and Belle were happy to be pulling something familiar—and they pulled the heavy car out of the mud at the same time.[17]

Vern Elefson, who grew up in Missouri, recalls another tale of horses saving auto drivers when the spring weather had turned the roads to mud. In 1927 road construction crews built a new major highway, U.S. 71, between Butler and Rich Hill, Missouri. About three miles of the road crossed some low land between two major streams. As Elefson remembers, "The year after the new road was built, the region received record amounts of rainfall and the bottomland flooded, covering the new road. The water covering the road was only six inches to a foot or so deep, yet it essentially stopped traffic."

The water was deep enough to make the new road invisible to drivers. A farmer living nearby named Sandy Silvers saw an opportunity. He shod the front feet of his horses, loaded chains and ropes on a wagon, and headed to the flooded road. For one dollar a car, he offered to guide motorists along the flooded portion of the new highway to high ground. He tied the cars together behind his wagon, sometimes as many as eight or ten at a time. Silvers relied on the click of the horseshoes on the pavement to keep the horses walking on the invisible road. When he finished guiding a string of cars through the flooded stretch, he usually found another string waiting to be guided in the other direction. As long the road remained flooded, Silvers worked twenty-four hours a day, stopping only long enough to feed his horses and nap when the traffic let up.[18]

Horses as Family Members

Frank and Charlie were Percheron draft horses, brown with tan manes and tails, each weighing about 1,800 pounds. They were already members of my family, along with Fanny, our big brown and tan, long-nosed collie, by the time I was born. When I was old enough to be curious, I asked Pa how the horses got their names.

"We named them after our neighbors, Frank Kolka and Charlie George," Pa said.

People living in a farm community knew the names of each other's horses just as well as they knew the names of their kids. They knew the horses' personalities, too. For instance, our neighbor Wilbur Witt owned a horse named Jerry—a big, lazy, good-for-nothing

A farm family and team stand in front of their Wisconsin farmstead, 1898.
(WHI IMAGE ID 1937)

Farmers like this one in Black River Falls, Wisconsin, were proud of their horses.
(WHI IMAGE ID 43393)

animal that would kick or bite you every chance he got. Ma would never call me Jerry—it was always Jerold—because she didn't want anyone to compare me to a neighbor's worthless horse.

Our team, Frank and Charlie, were geldings, or castrated males. This made them quite dependable, as their thoughts never strayed beyond eating, drinking, and trying to do their master's bidding. To Frank and Charlie a mare was just another horse, which was a good thing when you were hanging onto the lines and didn't want any surprises. Unlike the neighbor horse, Jerry, neither Frank nor Charlie ever tried to kick or bite me, but they did have some bad habits. By the time I was ten years old Pa showed me how to harness them. I was short for my age, so I had to stand on my tiptoes to toss the leather harness over their broad backs. When Pa was there watching, all went well. But Frank and Charlie knew when Pa wasn't around, and just before I tossed the harness onto either horse he would squeeze me against the side of the stall—not hard enough to hurt me, but hard enough so I couldn't put the harness in place.

I'd put down the harness, yell "get over" in my most authoritative ten-year-old voice, and slap the horse on the rump. The animal would move over, and I would continue harnessing him. This happened *every* time Pa was not around. It became a kind of game for Frank and Charlie and me, sort of a draft horse initiation for a farm kid growing up and learning the ways of horses and everything else on the farm. As I got older, taller, and stronger they no longer tried the "squeeze the kid" stunt nearly as often.

We had a third horse on our farm. Dick was a western mustang, black as a moonless night and unpredictable as the weather. He was considerably smaller than Frank and Charlie, weighing about 1,200 pounds. Pa had bought Dick to do light work, such as cultivating corn with a walking, one-row cultivator or snaking logs out of the woods in winter when there was three feet of snow on the ground. Dick was all muscle, and when he put his mind to it he could pull nearly as much as Frank or Charlie. But Dick and Dick alone decided how hard he wanted to work, no matter how much encouragement we gave him by way of yells and commands.

Another of Dick's never-changing behaviors was moving fast when he was pointed toward the barn and plodding along when he was headed in the opposite direction. For instance, if I happened to be cultivating potatoes in a field north of the barn, he'd poke along like he was pulling a threshing machine as we headed away from the barn. When we got to the end of the row and pointed back toward the barn, his ears perked up and he tried to trot with the cultivator—not a good thing, especially in stony soil. In his horse mind, anytime he was pointed toward the barn might mean we were through cultivating for the day, even if we'd been at it for only an hour or so. He wasn't lazy, just smart.

NOTES FROM

The Horse Barn

Horses are pretty good at expressing their feelings. When they are annoyed or angry, they lay their ears back against their neck. When happy and interested, they prick up their ears and face them forward. If a horse's ears are lowered slightly, the horse is relaxed, or perhaps bored. If its ears are flickering, the horse is listening and attentive.[19]

Pa didn't let me near Dick until I was thirteen or fourteen. Even then I had all I could do to keep Dick doing what he was supposed to be doing. Pa, on the other hand, developed a special relationship with Dick. Maybe it was because Pa had once worked on a ranch in South Dakota where they had twenty or thirty horses, many of them mustangs, and he had learned to respect what these little, often near-wild horses could do. Pa and Dick liked each other, and Dick had great respect for Pa. That little black horse would do anything for his master; he'd pull until he broke his harness if Pa asked him to.

Frank and Charlie were always together, whether they were in harness or in the barnyard or pasture after the day's work was done. They got along well with each other, depended on each other, and were never out of each other's sight. Dick was more of a loner, mostly because his coworkers ignored him, as he ignored them. All three horses

OLD DAN

Walter Bjoraker grew up on a farm near Owatonna, Minnesota. Now in his late eighties, Bjoraker remembers how important horses were to his family—indeed, they were members of the family. The family had a favorite horse called Old Dan.

Old Dan had become feeble, not steady on his feet, and was bumping into things because of near blindness. Dad decided he had to be destroyed. My brothers had ridden Dan. He had pulled their buggy when Mother attended Ladies Aid or visited a neighbor lady. In addition he pulled his share of farm implements. The decision that he must be destroyed had an emotional impact on the entire family, especially on me. I was about five years old.

At the time, there were no rendering plants or other ways of disposing of dead animals. That winter, as was common

practice in our neighborhood, Dan was shot and left in the hog pen until spring. This was another example of the difficult actions that were a part of farm life. In this era of salvaging anything useful, it was decided to skin Dan to make a robe as he had such a fine coat. Somehow, when the robe came back from the tannery with its glossy hair and warm flannel lining, it didn't hurt so much that old Dan was gone. In fact, as I with other schoolkids snuggled under the robe in the sleigh bringing us home from school in a snowstorm, and the robe topped the bedcovers in the upstairs bedroom when the temperature dropped below freezing in the room, Dan still seemed to be helping.[1]

NOTES

1. Walter Bjoraker, personal correspondence, January 15, 2006.

Unbroken western range horses, often called mustangs, were regularly brought to Wisconsin and sold to farmers at low prices. A farmer often teamed a mustang with much larger draft horses.

(WHI IMAGE ID 41801)

loved and respected Fanny, our farm dog; I often saw her in the barnyard, walking from one horse to another, wagging her big tail in greeting. The horse would bend over and sniff her in return. Frank, Charlie, and Dick surely looked like they were sharing secrets with Fanny, maybe even talking about Pa and me and farmwork in general.

Horses were much more than a source of power on the farm. Author and newspaper columnist Howard Sherpe interviewed Alf Tomtengen from Westby, Wisconsin, a bachelor farmer who was still working at age ninety. Sherpe asked him how he liked farming with horses compared to using a tractor.

"I liked farming with horses better," Alf said. "At least with horses you were never alone."[20]

Farmers spent countless hours with their horses as they farmed through the year. How profound to note that one was never alone when working with horses; another living creature was working alongside you, sharing in the labor and reaping its rewards, just like the rest of the family.

Plowing with a team of draft horses and a one-bottom walking plow at Wade House historic site, Greenbush, Wisconsin. Land was plowed in this way from the mid-1800s until World War II in many midwestern farming communities. After the war, tractors replaced horses, and the farmer's work was considerably easier.

4

DRAFT HORSES TODAY

By the 1950s nearly every farmer owned at least one tractor, and draft horse numbers had begun a rapid decline. In 1915 Wisconsin had almost 750,000 horses; by 1954 the number had skidded to 126,000, an 83.2 percent decline.

Clearly, when it came to getting work done on the farm, farmers preferred the iron horse to the draft horse. But when farmers switched from horse power to tractor power, many of them kept their horses. "Never can tell when they'll come in handy," my father said when I asked him why we kept the team long after we had tractors. And they did come in handy, toting wood out of the woodlot during a snowy January, pulling a tractor that wouldn't start on a below-zero morning, picking stones before we sowed grain or planted corn. Picking stones, in particular, was a killer job with a tractor—climbing on and off the tractor was harder work than lifting the rocks. But with a team, a shake of the lines and a quiet "gid' up," and the stoneboat moved right along.

Some farmers never bought a tractor. Some were just too poor to afford one, and others resisted progress. Weston Coombes, the farmer from whom we bought the farm I own now, never owned a tractor or even a car. He farmed as his father and grandfather had before him, never changing. It was a poor farm, and he was a poor farmer (by neighborhood standards). But he seemed to enjoy working with his team, day in and day out, season after season. When it was time to go to town, some four and half miles away, or visit a neighbor, Coombes hitched his team to his four-wheeled buggy, and he and his mother were off. Some people made fun of them—many even felt sorry for them—but they seemed happy to move along at a team's pace, seeing a countryside the rest of us missed as we sped along at fifty miles an hour.

Long after their neighbors drove cars, the Coombes family continued to drive a team on a buggy like this one. Weston Coombes and his mother drove their team and buggy to visit neighbors, buy groceries in town, and go wherever they needed to go. (SEARS, ROEBUCK CATALOG, 1908)

Green Lake Co.

An Amish farmer and his team spread manure on fields near Cambria, Wisconsin, in April 2009. (PHOTO BY MARK HOFFMAN, COURTESY OF *THE MILWAUKEE JOURNAL SENTINEL*)

Today's Working Horses

Some people keep horses for nostalgic reasons. They may have grown up driving horses, and although they eventually farmed with tractors, they always kept horses around. Orrin Schleicher of Mount Morris, Wisconsin, still has a pair of big Belgians named Barney and Smokey. "Don't do much of anything with them," he explains. "Look at them. Hitch them to a wagon once in a while. Put bells on the harnesses in winter. These horses are members of the family. Just like the dog. Had them for five years. . . . I would think that through the years I've owned a hundred horses."[1]

Amish farmers have always farmed with horses and likely always will, as they live their lives and do their work according to strong religious convictions that prevent the use of tractors, combines, telephones, electricity, and a host of other technology most non-Amish farmers take for granted these days. The Amish provide an excellent example of a culture whose farming methods have changed very little over the years. They till their acres with draft horses, they haul their milk to nearby cheese factories, and they travel to town with a horse and a buggy for grocery shopping.

A growing number of farmers are working with horses because they believe today's highly mechanized farming process is destructive to the land, wasteful of fossil fuels, and ultimately not sustainable. They argue that horses are homegrown power, enriching the soil with their manure, reproducing themselves, and providing a simpler, quieter, more fulfilling way of farm life. Prairie Farm Produce, a community-supported agriculture (CSA) farm in rural Baraboo, Wisconsin, uses horse power to till the garden crops it sells by subscription and at the local farmers' market. The farm's owners also operate a small sawmill where they use their horses to harvest the lumber, thus causing

Dean Jensen and his Percheron team haul hay to Hidden Springs Farm's dairy sheep, January 2008. (PHOTO COURTESY OF BRENDA JENSEN)

NOTES FROM

The Horse Barn

Approximately 95 percent of the draft horses in North America today are either Belgians or Percherons. There are several draft horse breeds popular in Europe but not found in North America, including Ardennais, Comtois, and Rhineland.[4]

minimal soil disturbance in their woodlot. And they use their team for horse-drawn wagon rides during their farm open house.

At Hidden Springs Farm near Westby, Brenda Jensen and her husband, Dean, farm seventy-six acres with Percheron draft horses. They milk more than one hundred sheep and make prize-winning sheep's milk cheese in their own dairy plant, part of what they call "an all natural, back-to-the basics, old-fashioned, original farmstead approach to farming and crafting cheese."[2] And Rich Purdy and Maureen Ash of River Falls use their draft horses to mow and rake hay and to plant, cultivate, and dig potatoes on their two hundred–acre certified organic farm named Baldur Farm. They also raise and sell Suffolk horses.[3]

While many farmers in Wisconsin and elsewhere have had to grow their farms in order to stay competitive, others have stayed small but diversified, adding side businesses and recreational opportunities to draw visitors—and extra income—to their farms. And from sleigh rides to trips to the pumpkin patch, working horses have a role in many of these agritourism efforts. Near Brantwood in far northern Wisconsin, eight hundred–acre Palmquist Farm is a getaway for those seeking Northwoods serenity and Finnish hospitality; horse-drawn sleigh and wagon rides are among the major attractions.[5] Olson Century Farm near Cashton features its Percheron horses in carriage rides for weddings and other special events and uses them for plowing and horse farming demonstrations.[6]

Olson Century Farm participates in another horse-powered activity seeing a resurgence: logging. Historically horses played an essential role in the upper-midwestern logging industry, especially in toting logs out of the woods. By the 1950s giant machines had replaced horses in the woods. By the 1990s these machines—diesel-powered, computer-operated giants—cut wood with incredible efficiency but also often did irreparable damage to fragile woodlot soils.

Just as the sustainable farming movement has a growing number of advocates, so does the practice of sustainable forestry. Jim Berkemeier of Timbergreen Forestry, in Spring Green, Wisconsin, is a strong promoter of sustainable forestry practices. He works with forest owners to manage their timber without using the huge diesel-powered logging machines that run on tracks and tear up fragile forest soil. Many of these landowners enlist the lower-impact efforts of horse-powered loggers.

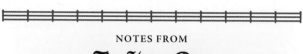

NOTES FROM

The Horse Barn

Assuming a well-conditioned team, equipment in good repair, and ten hours in the field, with two 1,500-pound horses, in one day you can expect to:

plow 1½–2 acres		**drill** 8–10 acres	
cultivate (single row)		**rake** 14 acres	
7 acres		**plant** 8–10 acres	
harrow 8–10 acres		**haul on a wagon** 1½ tons	
mow 7 acres		20–25 miles	

Four horses could accomplish twice as much with the same human labor but would require implements twice as wide.[9]

Any breed of horse can be trained to do logging work, but larger horses, those weighing 1,600 pounds and more, work best. Teams are generally used, but on occasion, when the land is steep, one horse does the job. The bimonthly journal *Rural Heritage*, out of Cedar Rapids, Iowa, offers an online Horse Loggers Directory: a list of loggers, including several in Wisconsin, who own horses and hire out to woodlot owners.[7]

As more and more people recognize (again) the draft horse's value for working the land in a low-impact, sustainable way, what other enterprises might soon be fueled by horse power? Writing in *Small Farmer's Journal*, Noma Petroff has urged, "We need to get the word out now that our nation needs its draft animals [both oxen and horses] if it is to survive in the impending post-petroleum era. If that can be done, it may prove a time with full employment, stronger spiritual values, and stronger community values."[8]

Petroff is certainly not alone in her belief that farming needs to examine the direction it is taking and make some dramatic changes.

HORSE POWER VS. HORSEPOWER

Looking for a lifestyle that gives you more time to smell the roses? Nothing will do that for you quicker than working your land with draft animals. While doing fieldwork you'll have plenty of time to notice the natural world around you, and without the constant smell of gasoline or diesel exhaust clogging up your nostrils. Sure, a draft animal will "exhaust" occasionally, but the brief odor only serves as a reminder that your soil's fertility is being boosted.

Teamsters who work their gardens, fields, and woodlots with draft-animal power cite many reasons. Among them:

Draft animals tread lightly on the land. Compared to machinery used for farming and woodlot management, they do minuscule damage.

They help plant and harvest their own "fuel," making you less dependent on fossil fuels.

(continued on next page)

Horses Aldo and Jed, driven by owner Maureen Ash, hill potatoes at Baldur Farm. (PHOTO BY BOB MISCHKA, COURTESY OF MAUREEN ASH)

HORSE POWER VS. HORSEPOWER

(continued from page 61)

They cost less than mechanized equipment (both to purchase and to maintain), they don't depreciate as rapidly, and they don't break down as often.

They work well in hilly terrain that defies a tractor.

They can work soil that's wet enough to bog down machinery.

They let you easily work without human helpers—a properly trained team will pull ahead on voice command while, for example, you haul hay, clear a field of stones, or gather up firewood.

Their slower pace gives you plenty of time to think while you work, making you less likely to get hurt in an accident compared to operating fast, noisy, powerful equipment.

They offer companionship. No one develops the rapport with a rototiller or a tractor that a teamster inevitably has with a team.

Lest you get the romantic notion that working with draft animals is nothing but a bed of roses, here are a few things to consider:

They require training. Even if you acquire a team that's already well trained, they need to adjust to their new teamster.

You, too, must be trained. Agreed, you have to go through a learning curve when you first operate a tractor, but with draft animals you never stop learning.

You need patience. If an animal doesn't want to, it doesn't want to. Usually there's a good reason, but the animal can't tell you what that reason is. You have to get into the animal's head and figure it out for yourself.

Draft animals must be worked regularly to keep their bodies in condition and to remind them of their training.

Draft animals, like the family cat or dog, require regular health care, veterinary checks, and vaccinations.

They need frequent hoof trimming, and maybe shoes. You can learn to clean and trim hooves yourself, but shoeing requires the skill (and expense) of an experienced professional.

Draft animals eat, even when there's no work to be done. You can't just drain the fuel and store them away for the season.

You have to be there—every day—to feed them, to exercise or work them, and to make sure they're okay. If you like to be away from home often, you'll need to find a reliable friend, relative, or neighbor willing and able to take care of your livestock.

Draft animals require land—land to live on, and land to work. If you have only an acre or two, you don't need a pair of heavy horses or hefty oxen, but you might do nicely with draft ponies or mules.

The bottom line is that working with draft animals involves a trade-off of expense versus time. Your rewards are the satisfaction that you are living closer to nature and the serenity that comes with taking more notice of the natural world around you.

Written by Gail Damerow for www.ruralheritage.com; used with permission

Horses have long been featured in community parades. In this photograph from 1910, a horse-drawn wagon carrying a maypole and dancers from the Kehl School of Dance turns the corner from Wisconsin Avenue onto the Capitol Square in Madison.
(WHI IMAGE ID 3158)

Parades, Shows, and Pulling Contests

Many of today's draft horse owners raise them for a different kind of work: appearing in horse shows, driving in parades, and competing in pulling contests. Nearly every rural community in the Midwest and in other parts of the country holds a festival to celebrate a holiday or some agricultural commodity important to the area. A parade down Main Street is often a featured event, with fire trucks, old tractors, riders on horseback, and teams of draft horses pulling floats of various kinds. These parades attract hundreds of people, many of them there especially to see the horses.

One of the country's largest and most spectacular parades is the Great Circus Parade, a major summer event held in several cities from 1963 through 2005 and revived in Milwaukee in 2009. Featuring rare antique circus wagons from Circus World Museum in Baraboo, Wisconsin, plus exotic animals, costumed performers, bands, and novelty acts from around the world, the parade is a celebration of the elaborate eighteenth- and nineteenth-century street parades that announced the arrival of the circus to towns large

A four-horse hitch pulls a circus wagon in the Great Circus Parade in Baraboo, Wisconsin, 2006.
(WISCONSIN HISTORICAL SOCIETY PHOTO BY ELLSWORTH BROWN)

Draft horse owner Mary Jane Swedberg of Oconomowoc, Wisconsin, drives her four-abreast carriage, with passenger Marcus Jordan, at the Walworth County Fair, 2005.
(PHOTO BY BOB MISCHKA, COURTESY OF JEFFERSON COUNTY DRAFT HORSE ASSOCIATION)

and small. For several years the Great Circus Parade even included a forty-horse hitch, an unbelievable spectacle: ten rows of four Belgian horses per row moved along the parade route, carefully negotiating the turns.[10] People came to see the colorful wagons, clowns, and caged wild animals, but many came to see the horses, shown off in their finest harnesses, clip-clopping down the paved streets of town.

Many draft horse breeders show their animals at fairs, including the Wisconsin State Fair in West Allis, local and county fairs, and a host of other shows throughout the Midwest. Clydesdales, Belgians, and Percherons are the most common breeds at these shows. They compete in halter class (the horses are led in the ring on halter alone and are judged on their conformation qualities—strength of legs, depth of body, brightness of eye, and so on) and in hitch class (the exhibitor drives a team of horses pulling a cart or wagon while the judge watches how well the team works walking and trotting and how well the team can back its vehicle). Prizes include ribbons, money, and trophies.

The Midwest Horse Fair, held each April in Madison since 1989, is one of the largest horse shows in the nation, drawing more than 50,000 spectators and 650 horses. The fair is operated by the Wisconsin State Horse Council, which uses fair profits to support the growth and development of Wisconsin's horse industry. Attendees can see all types of horses from saddle and carriage horses to draft horses, attend seminars on such topics as nutrition and horse health issues, watch horsemanship demonstrations, and learn tips from trainers.

Horse-pulling contests have been popular ever since a couple of farmers looked at each other's teams and said, "I think my team can out-pull yours." Today's horse-pulling contests are akin to major sporting events, with contestants traveling hundreds of miles to compete. The horses are usually hitched to a loaded skid and attempt to pull it a set distance. These horses train rigorously for their sport; their owners work them every day to keep their muscles and tendons in good condition and feed them a ration of oats for energy, plus minerals and vitamins and a ready supply of hay.

At one time almost every breed of draft horse was involved in horse-pulling contests, but now, according to the magazine *Draft Horse Journal*, 98 percent of all horses in pulling contests are Belgians.[11] Several states and Canadian provinces have horse-puller organizations, such as the Wisconsin Horse Pullers Association, with a primary mission of publishing a calendar of horse-pulling events and publicizing the results.

NOTES FROM
The Horse Barn

At the Hillsdale (Michigan) County Fair in September 2008, Roger and Schmuck, a team of Belgians, set a new world record in the heavyweight horse pull: an incredible 4,825 pounds.[12]

A horse-pulling contest at an unidentified Wisconsin county fair, circa 1936 (WHI IMAGE ID 40909)

Resources for Draft Horse Owners

The quarterly magazine *Small Farmer's Journal*, devoted to people seeking an alternative approach to modern farming, features articles on such practical topics as how to set your grain drill, horse-powered mulching, and harness repair. Published since 1976, the magazine says it is "Defending Small Farmers and Craftsmanship." Thumbing through it is like traveling back in time, yet its philosophy of remembering the best of the past and applying it today is one garnering considerable support.

There are a number of other publications and online resources for draft horse owners across the United States and Canada. Published quarterly in print and online, *Draft Horse Journal* (www.drafthorsejournal.com) offers a mixture of farming information and horse facts and includes a popular column, "The Days before Yesterday," with information about horses from an earlier day. *Rural Heritage* (www.ruralheritage.com), available both in print and online, calls itself "a bimonthly journal in support of small farmers and loggers who use draft horse, mule and ox power." Along with useful and entertaining articles on horse health care, breeding, training, farming techniques, legal issues of draft horse ownership, and myriad other topics, *Rural Heritage* lists draft horse events, auctions and sales, and resources and provides interactive forums online.

Clubs and breeders associations offer many services to horse enthusiasts. The Wisconsin Draft Horse Breeders Association began in the late 1940s and continues to maintain an active program for its members that includes draft horse sales and equipment and carriage auctions. Its membership is open to anyone "interested in draft horses and who enjoys the camaraderie of other draft horse enthusiasts."

The Wisconsin Morgan Horse Club (www.wisconsinmorganhorseclub.org) sponsors a Horse-Powered Field Day each year, featuring plowing and planting with vintage farm equipment, stoneboat and log pulling, carriage and harnessing demonstrations, and assorted displays and exhibits.

Of course, the best way to learn about and appreciate these great creatures is to see them in action. Luckily, a number of historic sites and living history museums provide visitors the opportunity to see draft horses at work, from plowing in the spring to helping with the harvest in fall. The Wisconsin Historical Society maintains horses and historic horse equipment at several of its historic sites, including Old World Wisconsin in Eagle, Stonefield at Cassville, Wade House Historic Site in Greenbush, and Circus World Museum in Baraboo. Stonefield boasts an excellent collection of horse-drawn machinery.

PART II

A Horse Farming Year

A horse farming year is not the same as a calendar year. It is measured not by dates and months but by tasks to complete. The year begins when the temperature warms and the snow melts. It ends when the last crop is harvested, the fall plowing is completed, and winter returns. That in-between time, those days from autumn harvest to early spring, is the quiet time when both farmer and horses rest, plan, have some fun, and contemplate the coming season.

The farmer's year is a progression of events, each year the same but also different, as the weather in large measure dictates what will happen and when. Some years spring arrives early, by mid-March. Other years April drags on with little change and scarcely any farming. It's the same with fall: an early frost puts a halt on growth and hurries up harvest; a late frost extends the harvest time.

Back when farmers worked the land with horses, the farm family and their team faced the farming year together. Depending on their ages, farm children participated fully, the older children helping with the plowing and tilling and the younger ones with picking stones, hoeing, and other less-demanding work.

For a child, living on the farm was educational—and a side benefit was getting to know one's father in an unforgettable way. Working under Pa's guidance, we farm kids also learned the nuances of working with horses, the skills needed for driving them, the insights to understand them.

While his city cousin with a factory job knew what his work would be every day, week after week, the farmer's work varied and was seldom the same for more than a few days at a time. For some, it was the unpredictable nature of the farming life that kept the farmer on the land, some years reaping considerable rewards, other years bringing disappointment. From early spring to autumn harvest, the farming year was constantly changing. Farmers would have it no other way.

Horses pull a cultivator through corn nearly too tall to cultivate, 1927.
(WHI IMAGE ID 49810)

Previous spread:
A farmer and team faced each new farming year with anticipation and hope. From preparing the ground in spring to the final harvest of fall, horses and farmers worked together, day after day. Along the way they developed a close relationship, respecting each other and depending on each other as well.
(OLD WORLD WISCONSIN HISTORIC SITE / WISCONSIN HISTORICAL SOCIETY)

Old meets new: a farmer shows off his Milwaukee grain binder while holding a cradle, the implement used for cutting grain before reapers and binders. (WHI IMAGE ID 59874)

CLOVERLEAF
MANURE SPREADER

5

EARLY SPRING

When I was a kid, spring came slowly to the north. It still does. You could feel the season coming before you could see any sign of it. Some old-timers said they could feel the coming of spring in their bones, but if you asked them what that meant, they couldn't tell you. They said it was one of those things you just know.

The first real hint of spring came when the relentless northwest wind swung around to the south one early March night. When you woke up in the morning and walked out to the barn to do the chores, the eaves along the barn roof were dripping. Now you could *see* the coming of spring, and smell it, too. The horses sensed it. The cows in the barn sensed it, especially the little calves bouncing around the calf pen, certain spring was on the way.

That first springlike day, after the milking was done, we'd turn the cows and the horses loose in the barnyard and they'd race around in the mushy, melting snow, their tails high. Like a bunch of schoolkids turned out for recess, the animals played in the remnants of winter in jubilant anticipation of the warmer season.

Usually this first introduction to spring was short-lived, as one last snowstorm would blast in from the northwest. But we knew winter was on the run and spring was in the air—no matter how much snow fell in mid-March.

Hauling Manure

By the third week in March in most years, the snow had all but disappeared, the frost had come out of the ground, and the muddy barnyard had dried. It was time to begin the spring work. The first big job was hauling manure from the manure pile in the barnyard to the field where we would later plow and plant corn. In those years before we had electricity (and an electric barn cleaner), we daily cleaned the gutters behind the cows and dumped the mixture of straw and manure on an ever-growing pile in the barnyard. No matter how much you loved farming and farm animals, shoveling manure from behind cows and horses into a wheelbarrow, pushing it outside, and dumping it on the

It's difficult to improve the image of a manure spreader, but International Harvester tried. This front cover of a 1910 advertising catalog for International Harvester's Cloverleaf manure spreader featured an illustration of a horse-drawn manure spreader surrounded by clover. (WHI IMAGE ID 22710)

Pitching manure into a manure spreader was one of the least loved jobs on the farm. (WHI IMAGE ID 9237)

manure pile was not high on the list of favorite chores. Nevertheless, it had to be done every day from early November to late March, when the cows spent their nights in the barn.

The size of the manure pile depended on the number of cows and horses a farmer owned. In fact, one could make a fairly accurate guess about the size of somebody's cow herd by looking at the size of his manure pile come spring.

The process of removing the manure pile from the barnyard was simple but mind-numbing, hard work. We hitched Frank and Charlie to our steel-wheeled manure spreader, which looked pretty much like a wagon, with steel wheels and a box. The back end contained metal blades that spun around, powered by a series of gears, flinging the manure in a ten-foot arc. Pa and we boys would pitch from the manure pile into the spreader with a six-tine fork. When the spreader was full, Pa got up in the manure spreader's high seat, took hold of the harness lines, and headed for the cornfield. When he got there he pushed the lever to put the spreader in gear and drove in a straight line so the manure was spread evenly.

Pa hated spreading manure on windy days. Driving into the wind was fine, but driving with the wind kicked up small hunks of straw and manure that would bombard him as he steered down the field. By day's end, he smelled as bad as the manure pile.

MANURE SPREADERS

Mention reaper, threshing machine, or even plow, and a certain romanticism emerges in the conversation. Not so with manure spreaders. There is nothing romantic about a machine that flings chunks of animal waste out of its back end. Yet the manure spreader was one of the most important inventions of the nineteenth century.

Farmers knew well the value of animal manure as fertilizer for their crops. By the mid-1800s agricultural scientists had discovered that manure contains three nutritive elements important for plant growth: nitrogen, phosphorus, and potash. Manure also provides organic material to soil. But farmers had no good way of hauling and distributing manure on their fields. They used ordinary wagons (sleighs in winter) and a six-tine fork for pitching the manure on and off. It was tedious, time-consuming, smelly work.

Several inventors experimented with machines that would make manure handling easier. In 1850 J. K. Holland of North Carolina developed a manure cart with an endless apron, which continuously moved the manure from the back of the cart to the front, where it dropped on the ground, little by little, as the cart moved along.

In 1865 J. H. Stevens of New York was the first to develop a wagon-type spreader with an apron that moved front to back. However, it was not an endless apron and had to be cranked by hand into position before unloading.

J. S. Kemp obtained a patent for a manure spreader in 1877. His machine included movable slats to move the manure to the back of the wagon and

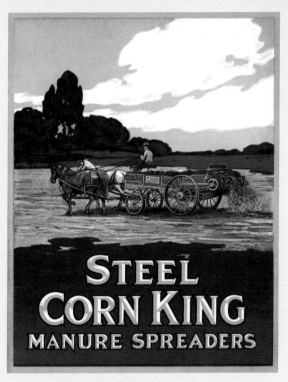

Cover of a 1913 advertising catalog for International Harvester's Steel Corn King line of manure spreaders (WHI IMAGE ID 23323)

a rotating mechanism that both pulverized and flung the manure in a uniform strip behind the spreader. Kemp's invention provided the basic mechanism that is still used in many of today's manure spreaders.[1]

By the early 1900s several farm implement companies were producing manure spreaders, including John Deere, International Harvester (which had purchased the Kemp factory and its patents in 1906), Massey-Harris, and the Moline Plow Company. The New Idea Spreader Company of Ohio became

(continued on next page)

MANURE SPREADERS

(continued from page 75)

From early November to March, spreading manure was a daily task for many farmers. (WHI IMAGE ID 47807)

one of the largest manufacturers of manure spreaders, making many improvements to the device.[2] International Harvester said this about its Corn King and Cloverleaf spreaders: "What is chiefly to be desired is strength and simplicity of construction. Strength is essential because a manure spreader has to carry a heavy load and the rear end—the machine end—has hard work to do."[3]

In 1908 a farmer could order a manure spreader from the Sears, Roebuck catalog. The Bonanza Wagon Box Manure Spreader was really a conversion kit for a farm wagon. Sears urged its customers, "Do not tie your money up in expensive running gears.

The Bonanza can be used on any ordinary farm wagon truck. Endless steel apron. So simple a boy can run it. So strong no load can break it. $49.50."[4]

NOTES

1. J. Brownlee Davidson and Leon Wilson Chase, *Farm Machinery: Practical Hints for Handy-men* (Guilford, CT: The Lyons Press, 1999), 192–194.

2. C. H. Wendel, *American Farm Implements and Antiques*, 2nd ed. (Iola, WI: Krause Publications, 2004), 296–306.

3. *Farm Journal*, February 1907, 93.

4. Sears, Roebuck and Co., 1908 Catalog, 542.

One or two of our neighbors either couldn't afford a mechanical manure spreader or simply insisted on doing the job the old-fashioned way, which meant pitching the manure onto a regular wagon, driving it to the field, and unloading by flinging the manure by hand with a six-tine fork.

Some farmers used a stoneboat for cleaning the manure gutters behind their cows and hauling the manure to the barnyard pile or directly to the field. Jim Erb's father, who farmed in Illinois, owned a Percheron mare named Nancy that went blind when she was seventeen. John Erb trained her to help with the barn cleaning, pulling the stoneboat behind six rows of cows. Jim remembers,

> *The horse would go through the door and knew when to move the stoneboat forward as dad pitched manure onto it from the gutters back of the cows. When the stoneboat was full, he would tell her to go dump it. The horse would go on her own behind the barn—she was totally blind—make a sharp turn so the stoneboat would tip, and dump the manure. Then she would come back in the barn and stop at the exact same spot where they had left off. The blind horse helped with barn cleaning for another sixteen years. Pa never had any trouble with her. He'd throw the harness on her and she'd walk to the stoneboat to be hitched. Of course, Pa always left the stoneboat in the same place.*[1]

Hauling manure took us the better part of two weeks, often longer. Blessedly, our country school was still in session, so my brothers and I usually had to devote no more than two or three Saturdays to this unpleasant but necessary task. Sometime Pa hired a neighbor, Weston Coombes, to help with the job, paying him the going wage in those years before and during World War II: one dollar a day plus a noon meal. When my brothers and I got home from school, Pa and Weston would still be in the barnyard, pitching yet another load onto the manure spreader as Frank and Charlie stood with their heads down, waiting for one more trip to the cornfield.

After World War II, Pa decided to add a few more cows to our dairy herd, which meant increasing the size of the barn. We bought another barn and moved it to our farm, attaching it to one end of our old barn. Pa arranged the new structure so that we could drive the manure spreader behind the cows and load the fresh manure directly from the gutters into the spreader. No more manure pile in the barnyard.

The Oat Field

Like most farmers in the early to mid-1900s, my father rotated crops—corn one year, oats the next, and hay the next. If the weather held in fall, meaning the ground didn't freeze until November, Pa plowed the former cornfield before the snow flew. (Most farmers preferred fall plowing for oat ground because freezing and thawing during winter would loosen the soil and provide a better seedbed the following spring.) In those days Pa planted between twenty and thirty acres of oats each year.

With the warmer days of late March or early April, the frost out of the ground, and the fields dry enough to work, Pa hitched Frank and Charlie to our disk harrow. Disking the field was the first step in smoothing the fall-plowed soil before planting. (Pa always corrected me when I said "plant oats." He said, "You sow oats. You plant corn; you plant potatoes, but not oats.")

Our disk harrow was only five feet wide, but it was about all the team could pull as they worked uphill and downhill, through the sandy spots where the machine sunk to the shaft, and over the clay knolls where the blades cut in only a few inches. Pa usually disked the field in both directions, following the plow furrows the first time and then cutting across the plow furrows the second time.

The disk harrow had a seat, so Pa could ride behind the team, which he did most of the time. When it was especially tough going for the team—on a sandy hill, for instance— Pa would walk behind the disk to make it easier for the horses. If the soil had dried quickly that spring, he rode in a cloud of yellow dust kicked up by the harrow blades as they cut through the soil.

CROP ROTATION

During the days of horse-drawn farm implements, nearly all farmers practiced crop rotation. The rotation began with plowing down a pasture and planting the field with corn. The year following the corn harvest, the former cornfield became an oat field. The next year the farmer would plant hay and leave it as a hayfield for three or four years. Then the field was likely a cow pasture for a year or two before it was once more plowed and corn planted. By rotating crops, farmers controlled weeds, insect infestations, and plant diseases and helped lessen erosion on soils subject to blowing and washing.

Not every farmer followed the same rotation plan. Some farmers planted rye and wheat in addition to oats. Many farmers in central Wisconsin grew potatoes in the rotation, as many as twenty acres when potato prices were high. Some farmers, especially during World War II, rotated in cucumbers and green beans as cash crops. On heavier soils, many grew canning crops, such as sweet corn and peas.

Disking newly plowed ground with a horse-drawn disk is a dusty, rough-riding job. (PHOTO BY STEVE APPS)

DISK HARROWS

The disk harrow, invented in the mid-1800s, used a series of metal disks to turn and smooth the soil after plowing, cutting and pulverizing it as it moved along. Farmers did not commonly use these machines until the late 1800s. Disk harrows, at that time usually pulled by two horses (sometimes three or more for the wider machines), included a seat for the driver, but some operators preferred walking behind the machine in the dust to the rough ride on the disk's metal seat.

Several machinery manufacturers made disk harrows. The J. I. Case Plow Works of Racine advertised its disk as "the greatest crop producing Disk Harrow made."[1] Other companies manufacturing disk harrows included John Deere, International Harvester, and Massey-Harris.

Sears, Roebuck and Co. sold a five-foot model for $39.50 in 1940: "You not only save as much as 30 percent when you buy a David Bradley Horse-drawn Disk, but you also get the best harrow that ever broke up a cloddy field. You'll be sure to like the work it does. All disks penetrate uniformly deep, from one end to the other, pulverizing the soil thoroughly."[2]

NOTES

1. *Farm Journal*, January 1907, 39.

2. Sears, Roebuck and Co., Spring and Summer 1940 Catalog, 939D.

Several machinery manufacturers made horse-drawn disk harrows, which were used to smooth newly plowed fields. Sears, Roebuck offered the David Bradley model in its 1940 catalog. (SEARS, ROEBUCK CATALOG, 1940)

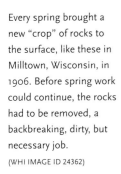

Every spring brought a new "crop" of rocks to the surface, like these in Milltown, Wisconsin, in 1906. Before spring work could continue, the rocks had to be removed, a backbreaking, dirty, but necessary job.
(WHI IMAGE ID 24362)

Once the disking was done, it was time to pick stones, the most dreaded of all farm tasks. No one has invented a satisfactory machine to do the job. Inventors tried for years to develop a stone-picking machine, but none worked nearly as well as a team of horses, a farmer, the farmer's kids, and a stoneboat.

As the last glacier molded the landscape of much of Wisconsin, it left behind a gift of fieldstones. Farmers in our neighborhood claimed that even if nothing else grew, we would always be assured of a good crop of stones each spring. And it was true—the freezing and thawing each winter brought a new crop of stones to the surface. To the artist, stones of various sizes and shapes, with colors ranging from reddish to black, were quite an attractive sight, perhaps even worthy of a poem or two, certainly a painting. But to a farm kid, stone picking meant days of dusty, dirty, back-breaking work that seemed never to end. There was always another stone to pick.

Fieldstones broke and bent farm equipment. They had to be removed before spring work could go forward. Why not work around the stones? Those few farmers who did were dubbed slackers.

It seemed as though stone picking always began on a Saturday in early April, when there was no school and when the nights were still chilly and the days rather dreary. With the barn chores done, we'd hitch Frank and Charlie to the stoneboat, and off we'd go to the oat field. Not an implement offered by any machinery dealer, a stoneboat was

Many Wisconsin fields were strewn with stones left behind by the last glacier. Farmers used horse-drawn stoneboats to haul the stones from their fields to prevent one breaking their farm equipment.
(OLD WORLD WISCONSIN HISTORIC SITE / WISCONSIN HISTORICAL SOCIETY)

blacksmith made and consisted of several white oak planks as much as three inches thick, eight or ten feet long, and sawed so the front end of the planks turned upward. The blacksmith bolted the planks together and attached a clevis (a curved piece of metal about four inches long) to which the doubletree was fastened. Our stoneboat had about a two-inch rim on all sides to keep stones from rolling off.

Riding on a stoneboat was a good way to practice balance. Pa held the lines to the horses, so balancing wasn't much of a problem for him. But my two brothers and I rode behind Pa, and we quickly learned to bend our knees and lean into the forward motion of the stoneboat as Frank and Charlie set out on a near trot toward the rock-strewn oat field.

Hour after grueling hour, we'd carry, roll, push, shove, lift, grunt, swear, and complain as load after load of stones found their way to the fencerows surrounding the oat field. We called these fencerows "shore," I suspect trying to be consistent with the fact that stones traveled there by "boat."

Our few tools for the job consisted of a crowbar, a five-foot-long piece of heavy steel an inch or so in diameter, a logging chain about eight feet long, and a shovel. If a stone was so large we couldn't lift it, we'd lever it onto the stoneboat using the crowbar. Occasionally one of us handled the crowbar while the other three pushed. When that didn't work, Pa unhitched the team from the stoneboat, wrapped the logging chain around the miserable glacial offering, and dragged it to shore, sometimes cutting a groove six inches deep in the soil.

Sometimes we'd come upon a stone we couldn't budge even with the crowbar. We'd dig around the edges, hoping the rock wasn't the size of a kitchen stove, and then try to pull it out of the ground using the chain and the team. When this didn't work, we ended up with a broken horse harness. Frank and Charlie would pull to their last ounce of strength, even if moving the stone was hopeless. Once in a while we'd just fill the dirt back in around the stone and declare defeat. Pa would mark in his mind the location of this permanent obstacle so he wouldn't hit it with the planting and harvesting implements.

By day's end, stoneboat tracks crisscrossed the oat field. To our imaginative young minds, the tracks seemed to have been made by some giant prehistoric snake, slithering around and around our oat field in search of prey.

The team slowed to a plodding walk as four very dirty, tired, and muscle-sore people returned to the farmstead, unhitched and cared for the horses, and walked to the house for supper. We were covered in dust from the tops of our caps to the tips of our shoes. For my brothers and me, stone picking ranked right up there on the list of heinous tasks along with forking manure out of the calf pen, cleaning out the chicken house in mid-July, and working in the haymow when the temperature under the barn roof was well over a hundred degrees. Unfortunately, clearing the oat field of stones after disking was only the beginning of what seemed like an endless spring job.

With the field disked, Pa or I drove the team on a drag, or smoothing, harrow, which consisted of three sections of four-foot horizontal steel bars about a six to eight inches apart, with six-inch-long steel teeth protruding from each bar. The drag harrow covered twelve feet of ground with each pass. A lever adjusted the depth of the drag harrow's many steel teeth, which further leveled the ground in preparation for sowing oats.

Of the many farm tasks, this one was about the dustiest. The steel teeth stirred up an immense cloud of yellow dust that swirled around the teamster who walked behind the implement. The team, out in front, was in the clear. Because the drag harrow pulled much easier than the disk, the team walked at a quick pace, making the dust cloud even bigger.

Back and forth across the field I walked. When I had finished the dragging in one direction, I dragged the field crosswise, to smooth it further. Then, with the dragging

SPIKE-TOOTH RUNAWAY

Working with a spike-tooth harrow could be dangerous. Vern Elefson, who grew up in Bates County, Missouri, remembers being twelve years old and working a field with a three-section drag and a team that at times could be flighty. Elefson's dad had broken one of the horses, named Fanny, only a few months earlier by driving her as the outside horse on a four-horse team, planting corn. The operation required sharp turns at the end of each row, which meant the outside horse had to back up a few steps to make the turn properly. If a turn with the fifteen-foot-wide—and very heavy—harrow was too sharp, the drag would lift off the ground.

Other than the flies and mosquitoes, which became vicious in the afternoon, the day had gone well. Close to quitting time—something horses seem to sense—the team turned too sharply. Fanny began backing up, making the turn even sharper. The harness lines went slack, and young Vern had no control over the horses.

He ran around to their heads to grab their bridles. Just as he got there, he saw the harrow lifting off the ground. The horses saw it, too, and took off running, scattering pieces of harrow, hitch, and harness over a quarter-mile as they headed for home. Vern had jumped out of the way and was not injured. When he caught up with the horses, they were grazing peacefully as if nothing had happened.[1]

NOTES

1. Vern Elefson, personal correspondence, September 18, 2006.

DRAG HARROWS

The earliest drag harrows were wooden logs pulled behind a team of oxen or horses. Farmers discovered that a wooden bar with metal teeth pounded through it provided a better and more dependable implement. Community blacksmiths made the earliest ones with oak bars and steel teeth.

Sauk County pioneer farmer William Toole described early drag harrows this way: "Nearly all of the harrows were of one pattern, shaped like a letter 'A' with a center piece extending forward from the cross piece. All were of wood, with teeth of ³/₄-inch iron, set without any slant. The number of teeth was about 17 to the harrow or drag. A few harrows were made with two side arms. This pattern gave room for more teeth, thus being more effective."[1]

Unfortunately, the oak bars could and did break when the implement struck a stone, a common occurrence in stony land like that in Wisconsin. Soon implement manufacturers were producing all-steel drags, and these proved popular for those farmers who could afford them. The 1897 Sears,

(continued on next page)

A spike-tooth harrow, or smoothing drag, as it was sometimes called, consisted of steel spikes set in wooden crosspieces. The device was pulled by a team of horses across a field that had first been plowed and disked. The smoothing drag was the last step before planting.
(PHOTO BY STEVE APPS, TAKEN AT STONEFIELD HISTORIC SITE)

DRAG HARROWS

(continued from page 85)

Smoothing a field with a team and a spring-tooth harrow, Greenfield, Wisconsin, 1935 (WHI IMAGE ID 23509)

Roebuck and Co. catalog sold all-steel drags priced from $7.90 to $14.00, depending on the size. The smallest drag covered thirteen feet, the largest twenty-six feet.[2] A local blacksmith likely could have made one for even less.

The spring-tooth harrow, another type of smoothing harrow, comprised a series of spring teeth fastened about a foot apart to a metal bar. The teeth dug more deeply into the ground than those of the spike-tooth harrow and would spring back from an obstruction, such as a root or a stone, without breaking. Farmers often used spring-tooth harrows to control noxious weeds such as quack grass, which required deep digging to get at the roots.

NOTES

1. William Toole, "Development of Farming in Sauk County: A Reminiscence," *Sauk County Farmer*, Middle of February 1917, 8.

2. Sears, Roebuck and Co., 1897 Catalog, 157–158.

finished, Pa once more hitched the team to the stoneboat, and we did another round of stone picking.

To help control quack grass in the hollows, Pa worked the land with a spring-tooth harrow, which dug deeper than the spike-tooth drag and would tear loose the tenacious quack grass roots. This wouldn't kill the quack grass, but it might slow it down enough to give the oats, alfalfa, and clover a chance to start.

Now, finally, the oat field was ready for sowing. Pa always drove the team on the grain drill. I don't recall that he ever let me sow grain until I was in college and we had switched from horses to a tractor. To him, planting the crop was a critical step with no room for error. One could miss a section of ground with the disk or spike-tooth harrow and it would make little difference, but missing a section of a field with the grain drill was a huge problem for Pa. I suspect his concern was mostly practical: no seed in the ground, no crop. But he was also concerned about appearances. He didn't want to face a neighbor who might say something like, "See you had a few problems sowing your grain field, Herm."

Before the oat seeds could be drilled into the ground, we would spend an evening or two in the granary with the fanning mill. This simple device, cranked by hand, cleaned the weed, seed, dirt, and chaff from the oats. The machine was made mostly of wood and stood about four feet tall, five feet long, and three feet wide. As one person shoveled the oats from the oat bin into the top of the machine, another turned the crank, moving the oats across sieves of various sizes. Smaller unwanted particles, such as weed seeds, fell through the sieves, and a fan blew off the lighter chaff and straw, while the firm oat seeds were shunted into a bag.

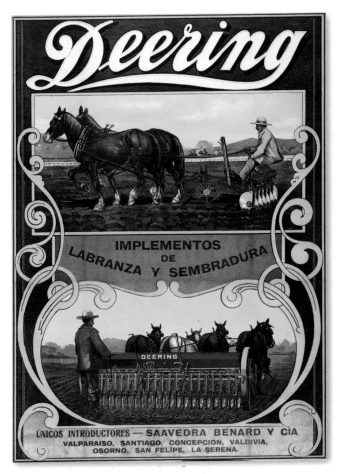

This Spanish-language advertising poster from 1913 features Deering horse-drawn grain drills and disk harrows. (WHI IMAGE ID 4358)

With the oats cleaned and bagged, Pa hitched the team to our Van Brunt grain drill and drove off to the newly worked (and stone picked) oat field. The drill's disks cut groves in the soil, and spouts attached to a grain box trickled oat seeds into the ground. Chains dragged along behind, spreading the soil

GRAIN DRILLS

For hundreds of years, farmers sowed grain by hand. Shouldering a bag of grain seed, the farmer walked up and down the tilled field, flinging the seeds from side to side, or "broadcasting." Of course, the skill of the sower determined the evenness of the sowing. Some farmers could sow grain as evenly as modern-day grain drills. Others had uneven grain fields ranging from no grain at all in some spots to too many seeds in others. A pioneer farmer described the process this way:

> On spring-plowed fields it was heavy traveling, for the man who carried grain and sowed by hand. Of course it was heavy work, even traveling over fall-plowed ground, with the grain hung over the shoulders, and the steady swing of the right arm throwing the grain as the right foot advanced and dipping the hand into the bag for another cast of grain as the left foot advanced.
>
> We sowed in straight lines, advancing toward stakes set at each end and the middle of the field. The stakes were moved sideways six paces. With this plan the throw in one direction was across what had been sown the previous casting. If the grain was not well spread, the growth would show in stripes lengthwise of the sowing. A side wind would also cause striped sowing. I used to overcome this difficulty by always swinging the arm in one direction to the side with the wind, using the right arm going one way, and the left arm the other.[1]

The first advancement in sowing grain was a mechanical crank seeder. The farmer still carried a bag of grain, but fastened to its bottom was a crank-operated machine that, when turned, uniformly scattered the seed as the farmer walked across the field. Several companies manufactured these broadcast seeders, some as early as the 1850s, and some models remained popular into the early 1900s. They were inexpensive and performed much better than a person broadcasting seeds by hand. After the farmer planted the seeds, they had to be covered so they would germinate. This was especially important for oats, wheat, and rye, which not only did not germinate well on top of the soil but were easy picking for birds. (In Wisconsin in the years before and during the Civil War, passenger pigeons descended on newly planted grain fields in droves and consumed enormous quantities of seed.)

Next, inventors attached these simple broadcast seeders to wagons and fashioned chain and gear systems that operated the mechanism as the wagons moved forward. Some of these early seeders were also attached to wheelbarrows a farmer pushed across the field, or were part of two-wheeled carts pulled by horses.

Jethro Tull, an English agronomist and writer, is credited with inventing the first practical grain drill in 1701. His machine sowed seed in uniform rows—and covered them as well, as short lengths of chain dragging behind the machine scattered soil. This freed the farmer from having to work the soil an additional time after the seeds were distributed.[2]

GRAIN DRILLS

As wheat became the crop of choice in Illinois and Wisconsin, farmers looked for faster and easier ways of planting their wheat fields. Then, during the Civil War, the number of men left to farm diminished considerably, and the old-fashioned seeders proved too heavy for many women to operate. An alternative to walking across a field with a broadcast seeder hung around the neck was now a necessity. Brothers George and Daniel Van Brunt of Mayville, Wisconsin, patented a design in 1860 for a combination drill and cultivator that was pulled by a team. The machine sliced a place in the soil for the seeds, placed them, and covered them.

By the end of the war the Van Brunt Company, then based in Horicon, Wisconsin, was well known around the world. In 1866 Van Brunt produced 1,300 grain drills. In 1911 John Deere Company officials approached the Van Brunt Company about consolidation, and the two companies reached an agreement. Now the widely known drill carried both the John Deere and the Van Brunt names. The factory remained in Horicon until 1970, when the company transferred its operations to John Deere's Des Moines Works in Iowa. John Deere manufactures grain drills to this day.[3]

By the early 1900s several other companies manufactured grain drills, including J. I. Case, Massey-Harris, and McCormick Deering. The Buckeye Drill, made in Springfield, Ohio, by the P. P. Mast Company, was popular. The company's 1907 ad boasted, "Buckeye Drills never disappoint. They are as perfect a piece of seeding machinery as you ever

This cover from a 1913 International Harvester catalog advertised the company's Hoosier line of grain drills. (WHI IMAGE ID 23321)

looked at. Sixty years the first Buckeye Drill was made and every year since they have been improved in every way possible."[4]

NOTES

1. William Toole, "Development of Farming in Sauk County: A Reminiscence," *Sauk County Farmer*, Middle of February 1917, 8.

2. "Jethro Tull (1674–1741)," *Encylopaedia Britannica*, www.Britannica.com/eb/article–9073727/Jethro–Tull.

3. Brenda Kruse, "Grain drills get going in the Midwest," *The Green Girl weekly web column*, January 15, 2001, www.bleedinggreen.com/GG2001.

4. *Farm Journal*, August 1907, 355.

to make sure the seeds were well covered. A smaller box containing alfalfa and clover seed sat in front of the main oat box, planting these seeds along with the oats. The oats and hay would grow together, oats serving as a nurse crop for the hay, providing shade from the blistering sun and preventing weeds from overtaking the fledgling hay plants.

Once the seeds were sowed, Pa hitched the team to a corrugated roller, a machine consisting of steel rollers and a seat for the driver. The roller packed and smoothed the seedbed, leaving little ridges in the soil that would help prevent it from blowing away on windy days before the grain crop had germinated.

With the oat field planted, we had no time for resting but instead immediately turned to preparing and planting the cornfield. The work was similar, except it included plowing, which unlike for oats was not done the previous fall. Stone picking, disking, dragging—the hard work of summer continued.

6

SOWING AND PLANTING

In May the cow pastures turned green, hayfields began growing, apple blossoms appeared, lilacs displayed their bright purple and delightfully aromatic blossoms, and oak trees began to leaf, beginning with a light green haze and then darkening as the tiny leaves grew larger.

Pa said, "When the oak leaves are the size of a field mouse's ear, then it's time to plant the corn." The whip-poor-will offered another reminder for corn planting, calling soon after sunset when the days began warming in May. The bird repeated its name, "whip-poor-will, whip-poor-will," over and over. Except Pa said the bird was calling, "plant-your-corn, plant-your-corn."

After the corn was in, usually about twenty acres, we turned to planting our cash crops—potatoes (an acre or two, except during World War II when we had as many as twenty acres), cucumbers (a half to one acre), and green beans (sometimes as many as two acres). In southwestern and southern Wisconsin, many farmers also planted tobacco as a cash crop.

International Harvester featured its McCormick-Deering corn planters, drills, and cultivators on this 1928 poster.
(WHI IMAGE ID 12056)

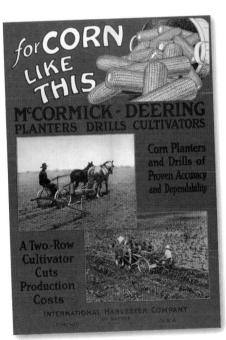

Corn Planting

As with oats and most of our other crops, we usually planted twenty acres of corn, sometimes a few acres more depending on how many pigs we had on the farm. The more pigs to feed, the more corn we grew.

Plowing was the first step in preparing the cornfield, where Pa had spread load upon load of manure earlier in spring. On our home farm, with its stony soil, plowing was surely the most challenging and difficult of all the tilling tasks. For many years, Pa plowed our fields with a one-bottom John Deere walking plow pulled by Frank and Charlie.

Plowing with a walking plow was hard work for both farmer and horses. Here a farmer guides a Chattanooga walking plow across his field, 1924.
(WHI IMAGE ID 48146)

By the early 1900s, horse-drawn two-row corn planters were popular in the corn-growing regions of the United States. McCormick–International Harvester was one of several companies manufacturing them.
(WHI IMAGE ID 46205)

Pa and his horses walked many miles in a day as chocolate-brown furrows replaced manure-covered former pasture ground, surrounded by the smell of freshly turned soil mixed with decaying manure. The sounds of spring filled the air. Meadowlarks called from the tops of fence posts; a gentle spring breeze rustled the emerging leaves on the trees and shrubs in the fencerows. The walking plow made a steady, subtle sound as it cut through the sod, and the harness leather creaked as the horses strained to keep the plow moving.

Pa tied the harness lines around his shoulders so both hands were free to guide the plow. In stony soil, a plowman knew to keep the plow handles in front of him. If the plow point struck a stone, the plow would leap out of the ground. Walking bent over the handles, as a novice plowman tended to do, often resulted in cracked ribs or worse.

The straightness of the furrow and how well the manure-covered grass was turned measured the plowman's skill. A well-plowed field was a thing of beauty, providing considerable pride to the farmer who labored mightily, especially on sunny May days. Pa rested the horses often on these warm days—often a chance to visit with a neighbor plowing in the field over the fence.

Art Swan, a retired farmer from Shell Lake, Wisconsin, recalls plowing with a one-bottom walking plow. "Once I plowed a thirty-acre field at another farm my dad had bought. The field hadn't been plowed for years. I was about sixteen then and it took me about three weeks to plow the field with a one-bottom, John Deere walking plow. The sod was so tough it didn't make a nice furrow. I enjoyed plowing, smelling the fresh dirt and watching the birds following behind me picking up worms."[1]

With the cornfield plowed, Pa hitched the team to the disk and leveled the freshly plowed earth. Then we picked stones again, and Pa dragged the field with a spike-tooth harrow, as he did before grain planting. And we picked stones again—stoneboat after stoneboat full of stones of every size and color, every shape and form. While we picked stones, my brothers and I were always on the lookout for arrowheads and for pieces of copper or something else the glacier left that might be valuable—or at least interesting, compared to the everyday run of fieldstones that seemed to be never ending in quantity.

In the Depression years, when money was scarce and hybrid corn had not yet become popular, farmers saved the best ears of corn from their crop, dried them, shelled them, and used the seeds for planting the next year's crop. Pa did this for years. A seed corn dryer stood in one of our unused upstairs bedrooms. It consisted of a metal frame with several rows of pointed prongs. Pa shoved the selected corn ears onto these prongs so the ears were lined up row upon row, but not touching each other. The ears air-dried

PLOWS

Early farmers in places such as Egypt and Mesopotamia discovered that to grow a crop, the soil must be disturbed. The first plow looked more like a hoe than what we today think of as a plow. This forerunner was really a crooked wooden stick that would dig into the soil as a person pulled it along. Gradually, farmers improved these primitive plows and made them larger. With larger plows, animals such as cows and water buffalo could provide the pulling power. By 1000 BC farmers in Egypt had further improved the plow by attaching a piece of iron to the front to make it sturdier and longer lasting.

There were few modifications to this basic machine until the Dutch made a substantial improvement in the Middle Ages by creating a curved moldboard that turned the soil rather than merely disturbing it.

During the colonial period in the United States, carpenters and blacksmiths built plows, constructing the handles, beam, and basic moldboard of wood and the cutting edge of the moldboard (the plow point) of iron. These early plow makers also fastened strips of iron to the moldboard so it would cut more easily through the New England soils.

A team plows with a sulky plow. To make the work easier for the horses, the driver sometimes walked behind instead of riding.
(PHOTO BY STEVE APPS)

PLOWS

No one was satisfied with the work of these early plows. They were clumsy, pulled hard, and generally did a poor job of turning the soil. Even Thomas Jefferson gave some thought to improving the design of the plow.[1]

Charles Newbold of Burlington County, New Jersey, received a patent for an improved plow in June 1797. Unlike its predecessors, Newbold's plow featured a cast-iron moldboard—no wood. But many farmers resisted, fearing that the iron would poison their soil and encourage weed growth. The claims were nonsense, but they slowed the adoption of this breakthrough plow design.[2]

Inventor Jethro Wood, a blacksmith in Scipio, New York, received patents in 1814 and 1819 for a cast-iron plow consisting of three parts. His was the first plow with interchangeable parts—if one part broke, it could be replaced without having to buy a new plow. The Jethro Wood plow worked well in New England, but settlers moving west discovered that the heavier midwestern soils stuck to the cast-iron moldboard and made plowing challenging.[3]

In 1833 Yankee John Lane arrived in Illinois and immediately began work on a plow that would effectively turn the heavy Illinois prairie soil. By this time blacksmiths knew that tempered plate steel on a plow's moldboard would scour, meaning it would become shiny and slippery and soil would not stick to it. Lane tried using an old saw blade but found curving it to the shape of a moldboard too difficult. He solved the problem by cutting the saw blade into narrow strips and welding them to a thin piece of softer iron.

As a busy blacksmith, Lane built plows only when a farmer wanted one, and unfortunately he never patented his important invention. His son John Lane Jr. took out a patent for a steel plow in 1857. He established a plow factory in Chicago in 1858 and made enough money to retire at age forty-five.[4]

John Deere is often erroneously credited with inventing the steel plow. Deere arrived in Grand Detour, Illinois, in December 1836 and set up a blacksmith shop where he shoed horses, fixed wagon wheels, and heard farmers complain about the difficulty of plowing the heavy Illinois soils. Apparently without any knowledge of John Lane's steel plow, Deere cut the teeth off an old saw blade and formed it into a plow moldboard. The local farmers were very interested in Deere's invention, and he built ten plows in 1839. Deere discovered that the shape of the moldboard made a considerable difference in how the machine turned the soil. In 1840 Deere made forty plows; in 1842 he made one hundred. He quickly expanded, hiring employees, advertising his plow in a local newspaper, and promoting the machine to farmers in the area.

In 1848 Deere moved his business to Moline, Illinois, and built a factory with the capacity to produce four thousand plows annually.[5] The John Deere Company went on to become one of the premier farm machinery manufacturers in the country, and it remains so today.

By the late 1800s many companies made walking plows, which were pulled by a team of horses

(continued on next page)

PLOWS

(continued from page 95)

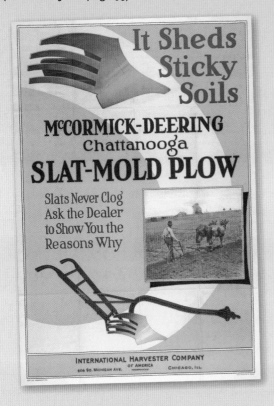

On this 1930 poster, International Harvester bragged that its McCormick-Deering Chattanooga slat-mold walking plow "sheds sticky soils." (WHI IMAGE ID 22921)

as the operator walked behind holding the plow handles to steer and keep the plow turning a neat furrow. The Frank L. Woodward Company of Clinton, Michigan, advertised, "Best one horse plow. Delivered at your railroad siding on receipt of $6.00 chilled or $8.00 with steel moldboard."[6]

After the Civil War, sulky plows began appearing, with wheels that would support the plow and its beam, and a seat for the operator. The Economist Plow Company of South Bend, Indiana, advertised its sulky plow as "Solid comfort. The wonder on wheels. Self guiding. Uses a wheel landside. Two horses instead of three. A ten-year old boy instead of a plowman. No pole. No side draft. No neck weight. No lifting at corners. Easier driving. Straighter furrows and lighter draft than any plow on or off wheels."[7]

By the early 1900s large manufacturers such as J. I. Case, Deere and Company, International Harvester, Massey-Harris, and Oliver were manufacturing both walking and sulky plows. A large number of smaller companies, many of them in the Midwest, made plows as well.

Plowing contests became popular events for farmers who wanted to show off their plowing skills and manufacturers who wanted to display their plows in action. In May 1866 the Missouri Agricultural

A horse-drawn sulky plow had two levers: one lifted and lowered the moldboard; the other adjusted the tilt of the plow bottom. (PHOTO BY STEVE APPS, TAKEN AT STONEFIELD HISTORIC SITE)

PLOWS

Two men compete in a plowing competition with horse-drawn walking plows, circa 1913. (WHI IMAGE ID 11494)

College sponsored the five-day Missouri Plow Trial in Columbia, Missouri, featuring the plowing skills of fifty farmers from six states. When the dust settled, the judges awarded first prizes to the Princeton Manufacturing Company of Princeton, Illinois, for a sulky plow in bluegrass sod; the Moline Plow Company of Kansas City, Missouri, for a prairie breaker in bluegrass sod; and the Speer and Son Company of Pittsburg, Pennsylvania, for a walking plow in bluegrass sod. The judges based their decisions on quality of work (25 points), adjustability (20 points), durability (20 points), simplicity (15 points), and draft (20 points).[8]

NOTES

1. J. Brownlee Davidson and Leon Wilson Chase, *Farm Machinery: Practical Hints for Handy-men* (Guilford, CT: The Lyons Press, 1999), 52–55.

2. Mary Bellis, "History of the Plow," http://inventors.about.com.

3. Ibid.

4. "John Lane and the First Steel Plow," *Lockport Free Press*, "Old Canal Days" Special, June 15, 1978.

5. Neil Dahlstrom and Jeremy Dahlstrom, *The John Deere Story* (Dekalb: Northern Illinois University Press, 2005), 13–26.

6. *Farm Journal*, April 1893, 86.

7. *Farm Journal*, February 1893, 37.

8. www.ag.missouristate.edu/cweq72b.htm.

during the winter. Mice that had sneaked into the house in fall constantly raided the drying ears and dined lavishly, except when they switched from corn to cheese and died when a steel trap slammed onto their necks.

In the spring, Pa shelled a test ear of dried corn and placed the kernels in a homemade germinator. He wrapped a certain number of kernels, usually fifty, in a moistened wet sock, close together but not touching. Then he rolled the sock and stuck it in a two-quart jar. He sat the jar on the back of the wood-burning cookstove—the warmest place in the house.

After a week or so, Pa would inspect the germinator to see how many seeds were sprouting. By knowing the germination rate, Pa knew how thick he should plant the corn seeds. He would hope for 80 or 90 percent, but depending on the previous growing year, the germination rate might be lower or higher. A dry spell in the previous year usually resulted in poorly germinating seeds.

We spent several evenings shelling corn to get ready for corn planting. With the field plowed, disked, dragged, and stone picked, Pa hitched a horse to a handmade wooden marker: a two-by-eight plank to which four two-by-fours, forty inches apart and about four feet long, were attached. The two-by-fours were sharpened so they cut an easily visible groove in the ground when pulled over it.

I'd never questioned why the rows were forty inches apart until recently, when I asked some old-timers about it, men who'd farmed with horses for years. "Answer is practical," one

HYBRID SEED CORN

In the early 1900s plant breeders began experimenting with a new concept, the production of hybrid corn, based on the theories and practical applications of genetics, which traced back to the work of Gregor Mendel, an Augustinian monk who experimented with plants. In his monograph *Experiments on Plant Hybrids*, Mendel described how various plant traits were inherited. Many plant scientists saw Mendel's book as one of the most important publications in the history of science.[1]

Simply put, following Mendel's breakthrough discoveries, scientists developed hybrid corn by crossing two genetically different corn plants, resulting in a new and usually higher-performing variety. Soon agricultural researchers were conducting experiments and field trials to select the best-performing hybrid varieties. Commercial seed companies began springing up to produce and sell the seed. Today, nearly all corn is hybrid corn.

NOTES

1. MendelWeb, www.mendelweb.org.

In 1940 Sears, Roebuck's two-row horse-drawn David Bradley Cornmaster promised "No 'double planting' . . . no 'skipped' hills . . . no 'scattering' when checking."
(SEARS, ROEBUCK CATALOG, 1940)

fellow shared. "Forty inches is the width of a horse's back end [he used another word]. If you're gonna move down the row with a horse, the row better not be any narrower." So forty inches became the accepted distance for all row crops: potatoes, corn, beans, cucumbers, and anything else planted in a row that required cultivation with horses.

Pa marked the cornfield in both directions, north to south and east to west, a procedure called "checking the corn." When he was finished, the field looked like a giant grid of hundreds of forty-inch squares. Pa would plant the corn where the marks intersected. Many of the Depression years were also drought years, but by planting the corn forty inches apart in both directions, there was usually enough moisture, so we got some crop in return. Following this system also allowed us to cultivate the field both lengthwise and crosswise, attacking the ever-flourishing weeds from two directions.

Pa's hand corn planter had a handle with a cylindrical metal container attached for holding the corn seeds. A shovel-like piece of metal made a hole in the soil in preparation for the seed. When Pa pushed the planter forward while it was in the ground, it activated a simple mechanism that released a corn seed. Then Pa dragged his foot to cover the seed.

By the late 1930s Pa had purchased a used two-row, horse-drawn planter with a seat for the teamster. This planter had its own marker, a disk on a metal pole that marked where the next row should go in the field. The planter's mechanism, not too different from the hand planter, released corn kernels at a set distance apart into a little furrow

CORN PLANTERS

For hundreds of years farmers planted corn with a hoe. They made a hole in the ground, dropped in a seed or two, covered it with soil using their foot, and moved on to repeat the process. This planting approach went on well into the nineteenth century. Of course, farmers did not plant nearly as much corn as they did wheat, rye, barley, and oats. A typical farmer in the Midwest in 1860 might plant fifty acres of wheat, five acres of oats, and two or three acres of corn, depending on how many horses, cows, and hogs he owned. Thus the push to develop a mechanical grain drill was much stronger than the incentive to invent a mechanical corn planter.

Iliakim Spooner of Vermont invented a hand corn planter and held a patent issued in 1799. George W. Brown had the first patent for a horse-drawn corn planter, which he developed in 1851 by modifying a horse-drawn cultivator. He patented his new corn planter in 1853 and started a corn planter manufacturing business. His Galesburg, Illinois, factory made six hundred corn planters in 1856 and one thousand in 1857; by 1878 his factory was making eight thousand corn planters a year. Other manufacturers stole his design, forcing him to go to court to protect his patent. The U.S. Supreme Court in May 1874 ruled in his favor and declared Brown the inventor and patent holder of the corn planter. The ruling also allowed him to collect royalties on all machines manufactured using his design.[1]

Machinery manufacturers including John Deere, McCormick, and J. I. Case began making mechanical corn planters. These could be pulled with a team of

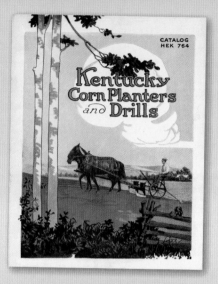

A 1913 International Harvester catalog featured the company's Kentucky line of corn planters and drills. (WHI IMAGE ID 23261)

horses, planted two rows, and consisted of a seed box for each row, a marker, a knifelike device that cut an opening in the ground, a mechanism that dropped a seed at specified distances, and rear wheels that covered the seeds.

In its 1908 catalog, Sears, Roebuck offered corn planters including a Kenwood two-horse corn planter selling for $22.25. The company also offered a one-horse corn drill, one that the operator walked behind. It planted but one row at a time and sold for $8.40.[2]

NOTES

1. City of Knoxville, Illinois, www.kville.org/kchistory/planter.html; *The* (Gatesburg, Illinois) *Zephyr*, www.thezephyr.com/backtrack/gwbrown.html.

2. Sears, Roebuck and Co., 1908 Catalog, 544.

the planter made. The wheels covered the seed with soil as the team, teamster, and planter moved across the field.

With this new planter, Pa abandoned checking the corn. The planter had a checking mechanism consisting of a wire chain with knots—although it didn't function very well in our stony and hilly fields.

The corn planter's row marking system did work well. With a little skill on the part of the operator, the corn rows were as straight as—sometimes straighter than—those made with the old-fashioned wooden markers.

About the time Pa switched from planting corn by hand to using a horse-drawn, two-row planter, he also switched to hybrid seed corn. Hybrid corn grew taller, could be planted more densely, had larger ears, and yielded more than the homegrown seeds Pa and other farmers had always used. With saved seed, the corn yield might be thirty-five to fifty bushels per acre; hybrid corn often yielded twice as much, sometimes even one hundred bushels per acre. (Today, some corn yields three times the yield of the saved seed varieties.)

Because of how it was developed, the seed from hybrid corn could not be saved and planted the next year. (Doing so would result in very low yields.) This meant Pa now had to purchase new seed corn each spring. A new crop of seed salespeople sprang up along with the new hybrid corn. They traveled from farm to farm, trying to convince farmers their corn was better, yielded more, withstood drought, and matured more quickly than homegrown seeds or their competitors' offerings. Hybrid seed corn was sold based on the days between planting and maturity. One could buy 110-day corn, 105-day corn, or even 85-day corn. The farther north your farm, the shorter the growing season and thus the need to plant corn that matured more quickly. Corn that froze before it was mature was as worthless as dry corn and sometimes couldn't even be used for corn silage.

Planting Cash Crops

When I was growing up during the 1940s and 1950s, cash crops provided an important supplement to the regular farm income from milk and hog sales. In central Wisconsin, farm families generally grew potatoes, cucumbers, and green beans as cash crops. From settlement days into the 1950s, growing potatoes offered extra income to usually cash-strapped farmers. Cucumbers and green beans came later. Farmers in western Wisconsin, especially Vernon County, and in the southern counties of Dane and Rock grew tobacco as a cash crop.

Tobacco fields like this one (circa 1874) were a common sight in parts of southern and southwestern Wisconsin.
(WHI IMAGE ID 26428)

No matter what the cash crop, it had to be planted in the spring. Cash crop planting competed with planting time for oats and corn (mainstay crops, planted for animal feed). Starting with the first day in spring that the land was dry enough to work, preparing the soil and planting crops became a frantic time, as each crop had to be planted at the appropriate time for it to provide expected yields.

Potatoes and Cucumbers

By the 1950s techniques for potato growing hadn't advanced much from colonial days. We prepared the potato field much as we did the oat field. In fall Pa plowed about twenty acres for potatoes; then he disked and dragged the land in the spring. He marked the rows with his handmade marker, the same one he used for corn.

Pa and a hired man worked up and down the long marked rows using hand potato planters. Each man carried a bag of seed potatoes over his back, rhythmically grabbing a potato piece, dropping it into the mouth of the potato planter, moving the implement forward so the seed went into the ground, removing the planter, stepping forward, and repeating the process, hour after hour, day after day, until they had planted the entire field. For days my brothers and I could hear the rhythmic clop, clop of the potato planters closing after each seed was pushed into the ground.

In the evenings, when the chores were done, Pa and my brothers and I gathered in the cellar of our farmhouse, sorting and cutting potatoes stored the previous fall to be planted the next day. We cut each potato into four or more pieces, making sure each piece included a growing eye (sprout).

Weeds began appearing in the potato field long before there was any sign of a new potato plant pushing out of the ground. Potato seeds germinate more slowly than oats, corn, wheat, or rye—and weeds germinate more quickly than just about any crop. Sometimes I'd come to believe the Divine punished us with weeds for our wrongdoings. Unfortunately, no matter how upstanding we tried to be, the weeds still grew, and quickly. In the midst of corn planting, one of us, sometimes me, often Pa, hitched Dick, our black mustang, to the one-row cultivator and walked up and down the potato rows. Pa called it cultivating the marks, which meant you treated the fading grooves in the ground as growing plants even though there was no hint of a crop in sight. If the cultivator strayed a bit, meaning you didn't keep Dick going straight, you might slice into the mark and turn up a potato seed—or several potato seeds—and note the whitish sprouts that were slowly working their way to the surface. When this happened, you stopped and carefully replanted the unearthed seeds, hoping they would continue growing—and hoping even more that Pa wouldn't notice later where potato plants were missing or stunted because their growth had been interrupted.

Cultivating with a one-row cultivator required learning. As when plowing with a walking plow, you tied the harness lines together and draped them around your shoulders. You pointed the horse between the rows you wished to cultivate, lifted the cultivator into its operating position, and said, "Giddap." Then everything began happening at once. The horse began walking, and the cultivator began moving. Steering

ONE-ROW WALKING CULTIVATORS

A one-row cultivator resembled a walking plow. Both had two wooden handles and a place for hitching horses. A walking plow pulled much harder than a cultivator and required at least two horses, while one horse—even a small one—could handle a one-row cultivator.

A one-horse, one-row walking cultivator. The spikes loosened the soil and dug up weeds between the corn, potatoes, or whatever row crop was grown. (PHOTO BY STEVE APPS, TAKEN AT STONEFIELD HISTORIC SITE)

On some one-row cultivators, the shovels (the parts that would dig into the ground) were narrow, useful for heavier clay soils; others had wide shovels, which worked well in sandy soils. Most one-row cultivators had an adjustment lever, so you could move the shovels outward to cultivate a full forty-inch row, or inward to work a smaller width. After our potatoes had come up and begun filling out and taking up more space in the rows, we adjusted our cultivator to

a narrower width. The shade of the potatoes killed the weeds closest to the potato plants.

A *Farm Journal* writer in 1893 made the following suggestions regarding a farmer's choice of cultivator:

> It should have small teeth and plenty of them. It should have broad hoe attachments for skimming the surface and cutting weeds; these are usually called sweeps. The width and depth of working should be easily and quickly regulated without the use of a wrench. As a rule the cultivator should run close to the plant while it is young, and, if the soil is compact, it should go down deep. Later in the season it should run farther away and more shallow.
>
> The frequency of cultivation must depend to a great extent on the weather. As soon as the crust forms after a rain it should be broken up by shallow culture. If the rain has been heavy and has compacted the soil it must be deeply stirred as soon as dry enough. It is an injury rather than a benefit to cultivate crops on wet, soggy soil. Weedy ground and frequent showers render frequent cultivation necessary.[1]

For many years farmers could buy two types of walking cultivators, a small one, pushed by hand and used mostly for garden work, and a larger one, generally pulled by one horse, sometimes two. Many manufacturers, small and large, made these implements. S. L. Allen and Company of Philadelphia advertised its hand-pushed model with the boast:

ONE-ROW WALKING CULTIVATORS

"A farm hand who could do five things at once would be a marvel, and yet two such men would not be equal to one Planet, Jr., No. 4 Hill Dropping Seed Drill. This machine opens the ground, drops the seed in hills or drills, covers it, rolls it down and marks out the next row. Does it all in the time a man would take to wet his hands. It can also be used as a hoe, a cultivator, a rake or a plow."[2]

Horse-drawn walking cultivators were relatively simple, with no moving parts and comprising a pair of handles, a spread of small shovels for disrupting the soil, and a place to hitch a horse. As recently as 1940, Sears, Roebuck offered three models of walking cultivators ranging in price from $6.85 to $8.65. The inexpensive model included five three-by-eight-inch reversible shovels, "of high carbon steel with reinforced points for double wear."[3]

NOTES

1. "The Cultivator and Its Work," *Farm Journal*, June 1893.

2. *Farm Journal*, May 1898.

3. Sears, Roebuck and Co., Spring and Summer Catalog 1940, 935c.

was the challenge. To move to the right, you pushed a little on the cultivator's left handle—the opposite of what you thought to do. Push too much, and the cultivator dug up potato plants; push too little, and you missed a swath of weeds growing close to the row. After an hour or so of cultivating, you usually got the swing of it, and barring the surprise of striking a stone now and again, the task could be quite pleasurable, especially on a warm spring day when the birds were singing, the trees leafing, and the grass greening up. The smell of freshly turned soil mixed with the smell of horse sweat and harness leather added to the experience.

Once the potato plants emerged, hoeing began. Of course, the weeds had a head start and were often taller than the newly emerged potato plants, so this first hoeing was particularly difficult, especially in the hollows where Canada thistle and quack grass grew in abundance.

As I recall, we began growing cucumbers in the late 1930s and beans in the early 1950s. We planted considerably fewer cucumbers and green beans than potatoes, no more than half and acre of cukes and a couple acres of green beans. Pa marked the cucumber rows with the corn planter, and we planted cucumbers and green beans by hand. The planting was fastest with two people doing the job: one person made the hole on the mark with the hoe; the other dropped in the seeds and covered them with his foot.

Once the plants had come up, we began cultivating the crops and hoeing, always hoeing. Hoeing felt like a never-ending job to keep our cash crops moving along, but unlike with potatoes, my brothers and I had a great incentive for hoeing beans and cucumbers. We received one penny for each bushel of potatoes we picked when we harvested them in the fall; if the potatoes were good, the men doing the digging were proficient, and we hustled along, we might pick a hundred bushels in a day and receive one dollar. But for cucumbers and green beans, we could earn as much as ten dollars from a day's picking, sometimes more.

Tobacco

I never worked with tobacco as a cash crop, but I've heard a lot about it from those who did. As with potatoes, cucumbers, and green beans, growing tobacco involved tremendous amounts of hand labor.

Although it was a temperamental, labor-intensive crop, tobacco became a lucrative business in late 1800s Wisconsin, particularly in the south and west.[2] Edgerton once boasted a major cigar-making industry and fifty-five tobacco warehouses.[3]

Most tobacco farmers grew one or two acres of tobacco, but some had as many as ten acres. The size of the tobacco patch was directly related to the size of the farmer's tobacco-curing shed: if too much tobacco was planted, there wouldn't be room to dry and cure it.

Planting tobacco required several steps, starting with plowing, disking, and smoothing the soil for the tobacco bed, a relatively small area where the tobacco seeds would germinate before being transplanted to the field. Once the soil was prepared, someone—often a neighboring farmer—who owned a steam engine came by and pumped steam into the tobacco bed to kill weed seeds and insects to a depth of six inches. Next the farmer mixed the tiny tobacco seeds with an extender that would help distribute the seeds evenly (some farmers used rotten wood from an old stump). The farmer spread the seed-extender mixture over the tobacco bed and covered the bed with cheesecloth, which provided warmth and kept out birds and animals.

Once the seeds germinated, the farmer plowed, disked, and harrowed the tobacco patch with his team. When the plants were a few inches tall, by early June, the farmer carefully pulled them, one or two at a time, from the bed and placed the fragile plants in boxes or wooden baskets. Next the farmer used his horse-drawn (later tractor-drawn) tobacco planter to set the plants in the ground.

The horse-pulled planter, which looked something like a corn planter, cut two V-shaped grooves in the soil. The two people riding the machine alternately placed a

Row crops were often cultivated with a one-horse walking cultivator.
(WHI IMAGE ID 49805)

A farmer surveys his tobacco crop, ready for harvest, in DeForest, Wisconsin, 1929.
(WHI IMAGE ID 2805)

tobacco plant in the groove and then held it there until the machine firmed it into place. A mechanism attached to a barrel of water discharged a cup of water for each plant as it was set. It took considerable skill for the men to time the whole operation.

After a week or so, the farmer inspected his tobacco patch and replaced any missing plants, on his hand and knees, one plant at a time. Of course, hoeing was essential, especially until the little plants grew to ten or twelve inches and began shading the ground, thus preventing weed growth. Cultivating between the rows with a one-horse cultivator was also necessary to destroy the majority of the weeds that grew rapidly in the rich tobacco patch soil. (Some critics claimed farmers put more manure on their tobacco patches then they did on their cornfields, and thus the tobacco patches had the highest fertility of any soil on the farm.)

When the tobacco plants were waist height, the tobacco grower and farm family walked the rows of the tobacco patch and cut off the top eight to ten inches of each plant, encouraging the leaves to enlarge—and, unfortunately, encouraging suckers (side growth) to form at each leaf junction. If the suckers grew to two to four inches long before harvest time, they too had to be removed.[4]

Cultivating Corn

Once our corn crop was up and growing, Pa hitched the team to the sulky cultivator, which was a vast improvement over the one-row walking cultivator we continued to use for cultivating potatoes. The sulky cultivator had wheels and a seat for the operator, plus it straddled a corn row, digging out weeds on each side. You could do twice as much cultivating with a sulky cultivator as you could walking behind a one-horse walking cultivator. Better yet, you could ride while you were doing it. The machine had foot pedals for moving the shovels back and forth to keep them lined up on the row, and it had a lever for lifting and lowering the shovels when the driver got to the end of a row.

Riding the sulky cultivator on a hot spring day did have its challenges. Charlie Sweet remembers when he was fifteen years old and growing up on a farm near Adrian, Michigan, about forty miles from Toledo. The year was 1938.

> It was a warm day in June, and I was cultivating corn with a one-row sulky cultivator. Our team, Andy and Min, a pair of Percherons, were pulling the cultivator as I sat on the seat. About mid-afternoon, my dad brought me some lemonade. He was waiting at the end of the row.
>
> It was warm, and after watching the horses' rear ends for a couple of hours, I must have fallen asleep. Anyway, when I got to the end of the row where my dad was waiting, I was not on the same row I started with at the other end of the field.
>
> The words used by my dad are not printable. After he left, I walked back along the row I had been cultivating. Someplace near the middle of the field, I had crossed over to a different row and took out a considerable number of corn plants. I blamed Andy and Min. They should have known better.[5]

Vern Elfeson, who grew up on a farm near Butler, Missouri, recalls a time he was cultivating with a one-row sulky cultivator. He was fourteen at the time. The cornfield was on the other side of a creek that cut through the farm, so to save time his mother sent his noon lunch out to him with his two younger sisters, Alice and Beth. When they arrived, Vern was on the far side of the field. The girls walked over to him and suggested they ride on the cultivator with him as he made his way toward the creek, where he would water the horses and feed them oats while he ate his lunch.

A sulky cultivator is not made for riders besides the operator. The girls crawled on the cultivator anyway, sitting on the crossbars between Vern and the horses. All went well until one of the horses glanced back, saw the girls, and became startled. The horse

This farmer has checked his field so he can cultivate the corn in more than one direction, circa 1910.
(WHI IMAGE ID 44688)

jumped, which caused the second horse to jump, and they were off and running, with Vern, two frightened little girls, and a sulky cultivator coming along behind.

To slow the team, Vern turned them into the rows of corn. By this time the cultivator shovels had dropped. As Vern said, "With the horses going at full speed, we raised a formidable cloud of flying dust and dirt clods!"

Vern traced two big figure eights in the cornfield. By this time the horses had tired, and Vern was able to stop them. He and his sisters crawled off the cultivator, safe and sound. The cornfield suffered most from the incident.[6]

Even though sulky cultivators became popular soon after their invention, many farmers continued cultivating corn with a one-row, walking cultivator. In fact, using that type of cultivator was often one of the first jobs for a farm kid. Orrin Schleicher of Waushara County, Wisconsin, remembers cultivating corn when he was six or seven years old. "I cultivated with a walking cultivator," he said. "I dug up quite a few corn plants before I learned how to do it."[7]

Once we had planted the corn and the cash crops, some of the hurry-up pressure was off. In mid-Wisconsin, the growing season—frost-free days—is seldom more than 120 days, a few years more and some years less. This information is especially critical for the corn crop, as the new hybrid varieties require 100 days and more to mature,

SULKY CULTIVATORS

In the language of farm machinery, *sulky* refers to a machine with two wheels. A sulky cultivator, pulled by two horses, had a seat for the operator and two sets of shovels for turning under weeds. The machine straddled the row so the shovels moved on each side. For newly emerging crops, the machine also included metal shields that prevented the soil disturbed by the cultivator shovels from burying the tiny corn plants.

In the late 1800s several machinery manufactures began making sulky cultivators. Many farmers, accustomed to cultivating with a one-horse cultivator, were reluctant to switch to the more expensive two-horse, riding machines. The manufacturers came up with a host of creative names to help sway these hesitant buyers: Joy Rider, Jack Rabbit, Uncle Sam, and Champion.[1]

The cost difference between a walking cultivator and a sulky cultivator was significant. In 1908 a Sears, Roebuck one-row walking cultivator sold for $3.87, while a six-shovel sulky cultivator cost $24.15.[2]

NOTES

1. Ronald Stokes Barlow, *300 Years of Farm Implements and Machinery: 1630–1930* (Iola, WI: Krause Publications, 2003), 55.

2. Sears, Roebuck and Co., 1908 Catalog, 548.

depending on the variety. (One could buy hybrid corn with maturity dates ranging from 85 to 115 days. The longer the maturity time, the larger the yield.)

By mid-June it was time to start haying, a more fun time than the planting season. Maybe it was the appealing smell of curing hay, or the sense of accomplishment when the barn's haymow began filling, or driving Frank and Charlie on a hay wagon to and from the hay field—these things I remember fondly, although the work remained hard and demanding.

For many years Wisconsin farmers, like these near Wild Rose, hauled loose hay from the field with their teams, piling the hay high on specially designed hay wagons. (WHI IMAGE ID 55557)

HAYING SEASON

By June we'd finished planting the potatoes and corn, and Pa began watching the hay fields. With ample rains in April and May, the alfalfa, clover, and timothy hay mixture soon reached knee high. Just as the clover and alfalfa plants began to flower, Pa declared it time to cut hay. He hitched the team to the hay mower and headed for the hay field.

Our mower was a five-foot cut McCormick with steel wheels and a metal seat. It consisted of a sickle bar with protruding spikes, called guards, there to protect the triangular knives, which sliced like shears through the thick growing hay crop and left it to dry in the sun.

The chatter of the hay mower broke the silence of the dewy morning as Pa slowly worked his way around the field, being careful at the corners to turn the team so no standing hay would remain. Soon the sweet smell of drying alfalfa and clover filled the air. If the hay mixture happened to include a little sweet clover, the smell was even stronger, but not in any way unpleasant. For farmers, drying hay is their perfume. Nothing compares to its sweet smell.

If the day was sunny and warm, the hay we cut in the morning could be raked by mid-afternoon. The hay had to be partially dry before raking, but not too dry, or the rake would shatter the leaves, losing much of the hay's nutrients. Once the field was cut, Pa hitched Frank and Charlie to the dump rake, which had two high wheels, a seat for a rider, and a series of curved tines that could be lowered and lifted. As the rake moved around the hay field, Pa dumped the hay accumulated in front of the machine by pushing a foot-operated lever. Soon the raked hay lay in horizontal rows, continuing to dry in the warm spring sun.

Then came the tedious part of the haymaking process. My brothers and I, each armed with a three-tine fork, piled the hay into bunches about four feet high and as many feet across. These little bunches looked like miniature haystacks; some folks called them haycocks. The bundles had to be carefully constructed so they would shed rain and would stand up to a strong wind.

Cutting hay with a horse-
drawn sickle mower, 1931
(WHI IMAGE ID 46741)

Making the first dozen or so hay bunches was fun, as it was a bit of a challenge to construct them properly. The next dozen were far less interesting, and the next one hundred were boring, repetitious, and mind numbing. To make the time pass more quickly, I allowed my mind to wander. I thought about school, what Ma had planned for dinner, or, by the time I was fourteen or so, one of the cute neighbor girls. As the sun climbed toward high noon, hunger trumped even girls. Only Pa had a watch, so my brothers and I were always guessing the time and how much longer before we could eat. We didn't dare ask Pa; he would think we weren't paying attention to our work. We surely didn't want him to know hunger was all we had on our minds in the hour or so before noon.

We brought along a brown pottery water jug with a stopper made from a corn cob. We shoved the gallon jug under a hay bunch to keep it away from the hot rays of the sun, but after an hour or so of making bunches, we usually couldn't find the jug because every hay bunch looked like every other hay bunch. Once found, the water was warm, but as Pa said, "It's wet." Even warm water was welcome as sweat poured off us.

HAY MOWERS

Before the mechanical mower became popular, farmers cut hay with a sickle and later a scythe, a tedious and backbreaking job. When farmers began raising more livestock, especially dairy cattle, the requirement for good hay increased dramatically, and the need to cut it quickly and effectively became paramount.

Enter the horse-drawn mechanical hay mower. Inventors who worked on developing reapers invariably also worked on hay mowers. The two types of machines had several similarities, although the reaper was the more complicated. (See page 134 for more about reapers.)

Inventors developed several early reapers as combination machines; with a little adjustment, they would cut either grain or grass. As was usually the case with such multipurpose machines, they did neither task well. In 1812 Peter Gaillard of Lancaster, Pennsylvania, patented a machine designed to cut only grass. Ten years later Jeremiah Bailey of Chester County, Pennsylvania, patented his grass-cutting mower, which was described this way: "Extensively used and approved of during the last season in the neighborhood of the patentee, and promises to be of great public utility. It is understood that it will mow ten acres per day."[1]

William F. Ketchum's hay mower, patented on July 10, 1847, was a side-cut machine and included a sickle bar with steel fingers driven by a single large steel wheel. The mower was pulled by a team of horses and had a seat for the operator.[2] Improvements on the implement were made over the years,

Buckeye's mower/reaper with self-raker was designed to cut both hay and grain. (WHI IMAGE ID 11851)

but the basic design changed little. J. I Case, the Deering Harvester Company, John Deere, and many others manufactured hay mowers.

A writer for an 1893 issue of *Farm Journal* magazine offered this advice for a farmer and his hay mower:

(continued on next page)

HAY MOWERS

(continued from page 115)

A modern mower cutting a five-foot swath can be drawn by a team of average weight. Haying time is too precious to be wasted by using a short bar machine. No time is lost by stopping to sharpen a dull sickle. . . . Keep the cutter bar well up for the sake of the knives, the team, and next year's hay crop. Keep the sections of the sickle riveted tight and all the bolts screwed up, and save a general breakdown.

The man who is always sure it will rain before night lets his grass get overripe and cuts it just in time to catch the storm. The wise man doesn't worry, but keeps his 'weather eye' open, begins haying before all his grass is ripe enough, runs his mower only when the dew or rain has entirely dried off of it, cures it mostly in the windrow, and puts it in the mow before it has lost all of its grassy color and aroma. . . . Don't forget to take out the oil can and the water jug with you to the field—no other jug needed. A little and often is a good rule for using both.[3]

NOTES

1. R. L. Ardrey, *American Agricultural Implements* (Chicago: R. L. Ardrey, 1894), 78.

2. J. Brownlee Davidson and Leon Wilson Chase, *Farm Machinery: Practical Hints for Handy-men* (Guilford, CT: The Lyons Press, 1999), 163.

3. "In the Hay Field," *Farm Journal*, June 1893, 128.

For all its downsides, bunching hay was one of those tasks where you could immediately see the result of your efforts. At the end of the day, when a ten- or twenty-acre field was dotted with hay bunches, Pa would take time to look at what we had done. "Isn't that something to see?" he would say. He saw beauty in a job well done that we kids couldn't yet appreciate. My tired arms and back and hungry stomach just wanted to get on home so we could do the barn chores and file into the house for supper.

After a day or so of drying the hay in the field, we began hauling the bunches to the barn with our steel-wheeled wagon. Pa always made sure the hay had dried well before we stored it, picking it up, crushing it in his hands, and smelling it. If it still contained too much moisture, there was danger of spontaneous combustion— the hay could catch fire and burn the barn. Every year we heard of barn fires caused by green hay.

On the other hand, waiting too long to haul the hay to the barn resulted in a loss of hay leaves and thus many nutrients. Plus there was the danger of the hay being rained on. The last thing we wanted during haying season was a couple of rainy days. If this

happened, we had to spread out the hay bunches in the field so it would dry. Wet hay in the barn turned into moldy hay, which the animals would not eat.

When Pa determined the hay was ready and when the morning dew had dried, we lifted the wide hay rack onto our steel-wheeled wagon, hitched up the team, and were off to the hay field. The procedure was simple. One person rode on the wagon, drove the team from hay bunch to hay bunch, and "made the load," which meant moving the hay around the hayrack so it could be hauled to the barn without risk of the hay tipping off or the entire load tipping over. Both of these minor catastrophes happened on occasion.

The most common of these incidents occurred when the teamster drove along a too-steep side hill and tipped the load. My brothers and I soon learned that a hay wagon, especially a loaded one, was meant to go up and down—not along—steep hills. The key was guessing which hills were too steep.

Farmers pitch loose hay with three-tined pitchforks onto a high-wheeled, horse-drawn hay wagon, circa 1915. (WHI IMAGE ID 46943)

HAY RAKES

Before the invention of hay mowers and mechanical hay rakes, a farmer raked the dried, cut hay with a wooden hand rake and piled it into bunches with a wooden pitchfork for drying.

By the late 1800s many manufacturers had mechanical dump rakes on the market. Walter Abbott Wood, a New York farmer, inventor, and machinery manufacturer, is credited with inventing one of the first functional dump rakes, circa 1853. The Walter Wood rake had spring teeth and wooden frames and wheels. The rake included a hand-powered lift lever that raised and lowered the steel tines.[1]

Soon manufacturers made dump rakes entirely of steel with a power-assisted dumping mechanism. The operator needed only to push a foot-operated lever, and the tines lifted and lowered. Dump rakes

remained on the market for many years as the Depression and World War II slowed down the mechanization of hay making.

The Sears, Roebuck catalog for spring and summer 1940 offered dump rakes in sizes from eight feet to twelve feet wide, with from twenty-one to forty spring teeth. Regular equipment included with the rake: "Combination shaft and pole for one or two horses; tractor hitch optional. Neck yoke and eveners not furnished." Depending on size, prices ranged from $35.90 for the eight-foot model to $47.25 for the twelve-footer.[2]

Mechanical hay loaders and side-delivery rakes appeared at the same time, by the early 1900s. The mechanical hay loader, pulled behind a wagon, required that the hay be raked into long windrows instead of individual bunches. Manufacturers

Dump rake (SEARS, ROEBUCK CATALOG, 1940)

HAY RAKES

Side-delivery rake (SEARS, ROEBUCK CATALOG, 1940)

perfected side-delivery rakes by the 1890s. As the name suggests, this machine delivered the raked hay in a long rope at one side of the machine. Thus, the hay could be easily picked up by a mechanical hay loader or a portable hay baler. John Deere, McCormick Deering, J. I. Case, Massey-Harris, New Idea, and others manufactured both side-delivery rakes and mechanical hay loaders.

As was often the case with new labor-saving farm equipment, side-delivery rakes cost more than the simpler dump rakes. But most farmers were willing to pay more for a machine if it required less manual labor and did the job more quickly. For instance, in 1940 Sears, Roebuck offered a horse-pulled dump rake for $34.90, while a side-delivery rake sold for $91.50, nearly three times as much. (And, while the Sears hay loader cost $129.95 that year, a three-tine hayfork with "oil tempered spring steel tines. Bronzed head. Bent ash handle" sold for seventy-five cents.)[3]

NOTES

1. Virtual American Biographies, "Walter Abbott Wood," www.famousamericans.net/walterabbottwood; Ronald Stokes Barlow, *300 Years of Farm Implements and Machinery, 1630–1930* (Iola, WI: Krause Publications, 2003), 64.

2. Sears, Roebuck and Co., Spring and Summer Catalog 1940, 947.

3. Ibid., 927, 947–948.

With one person on the wagon, the rest of us tossed hay onto the wagon with three-tine pitchforks. In those days, we each had our own three-tine fork, and no one would dare use someone else's. The handle on my fork and on Pa's was a foot or so longer than the handles on the forks of my brothers, who were younger and smaller. With a longer handle, I could toss about half a bunch of hay clear to the top of a nearly loaded wagon. As I did so, dry alfalfa leaves struck me in the face and sifted down my sweaty neck, causing an overwhelming need to scratch, which I could not do with a fork full of hay held high over my head.

Shortly after the end of World War II, Pa bought a mechanical hay loader, which eliminated the need to pitch bunches of hay onto the hay wagon. The hay loader changed other haymaking practices as well. As was more and more often the case, we needed other new equipment for the new hay loader to work. The mechanical hay loader required that we rake the hay in long, ropelike rows, winding around the field. Our old dump rake gathered the hay in separate, vertical clumps that the new loader could not pick up.

So Pa bought a side-delivery rake. Now, after the hay was raked, we hitched the new hay loader, which stood about ten feet tall and was six feet wide, to the back of the hay wagon.

Pa drove the team, straddling the long strand of hay left by the side-delivery rake. The hay loader's long reciprocating arms lifted the hay from the ground to where it tumbled off the top of the loader onto the wagon. My brothers and I moved the hay around the wagon with our three-tine forks, making the load. No more hours under the hot summer sun forking hay into little bunches. No pitching of hay bunches over our heads with hay leaves streaming down our sweating bodies.

Occasionally the hay loader brought up a nest of bees that had found a home in the raked hay. We boys would jump off the wagon and run, while Pa hoped the angry bees wouldn't take after the horses and cause havoc. Pine and garter snakes sometimes found convenient homes under the raked hay, too, and they came tumbling from the arms of the loader onto the wagon, hissing and upset. Again my brothers and I would jump off the wagon and run, leaving Pa with the partial load of hay, the team, and an unhappy snake. He'd grab one of the left-behind three-tine forks and toss the snake off the load; then he'd yell to us to come back, and we'd continue loading.

When the wagon was fully loaded with hay, Pa drove it to the barn for unloading. We would always stop by the pump house and dash inside for a drink of cool, fresh well water. Once in the morning and once in the afternoon, we enjoyed bottles of root beer made by Pa and Ma several weeks earlier using a Hires root beer extract. Stored on shelves in the farmhouse cellar, the root beer was cool, pleasant to taste, and a real treat.

MECHANICAL HAY LOADERS

In the late 1800s the Keystone Company of Sterling, Illinois, began manufacturing mechanical hay loaders. The ad proclaimed, "This is the Keystone Hay Loader, which loads hay from the windrow or direct from the swath where the hay is heavy. It greatly facilitates the operation and reduces the cost of harvesting a crop of hay. You can be short of help if you have one of these loaders because one man can load hay with it."[1]

The Keystone Company advertised its side-delivery rakes as a companion to its hay loader. "This side-delivery hay rake . . . leaves the hay in a light, loose windrow, where it is cured by the action of the air, and not bleached by sun; hay retains its bright green color and the essential oils."[2] In 1905 the J. I. Case Company of Racine, Wisconsin, added the Keystone hay loader and side-delivery rake to its product line of haymaking equipment.[3]

By the early 1900s several companies made hay loaders, including John Deere, Massey-Harris, Moline Plow Company, and New Idea.[4] Mechanical hay loaders remained popular until the 1950s, when farmers began switching from loose hay to baled hay.

$129.95
$10 DOWN

The mechanical hay loader replaced a farmer with a long-handled three-tined fork pitching the hay onto the wagon by hand. (SEARS, ROEBUCK CATALOG, 1940)

NOTES

1. *Farm Journal*, June 1898, 153.

2. *Farm Journal*, May 1898, 120.

3. Ronald Stokes Barlow, *300 Years of Farm Implements and Machinery, 1630–1930* (Iola, WI: Krause Publications, 2003), 67; "Case IH History," www.caseih.com.

4. C. H. Wendel, *Encyclopedia of American Farm Implements and Antiques* (Iola, WI: Krause Publications, 2004), 211–213.

HAY CARRIERS

Left: A farmer uses a mechanical hay carrier to lift loose hay from the wagon and deliver it into the barn's haymow, circa 1926. (WHI IMAGE ID 24267)

Above: Hay carriers comprised a series of ropes and pulleys that moved hay from a hay wagon into a barn's haymow. (SEARS, ROEBUCK CATALOG, 1908)

Before the 1860s farmers pitched hay into their barn storage areas with three-tine forks and backbreaking labor. In 1867 a young Iowa inventor, William Louden, improved on earlier hay-carrier models; his carrier lifted the hay perpendicularly from the load and then shunted it onto a track over the haymow, where the hay could be dropped at any location. This greatly reduced the hand labor required in the haymow.[1]

The basic hay-carrier system consisted of a track in the ceiling of the barn, plus ropes, pulleys, and the hayfork itself. The system was simple and relatively inexpensive. In 1908 a farmer could order from the Sears, Roebuck catalog a complete hay-carrier system for $11.05 to $16.60, depending on the size of the barn. The farmer received "1 steel track hay carrier, 1 short tine double harpoon hayfork, 30 feet of double angle steel track, 12 rafter brackets, 12 steel track hanging hooks, 4 floor hooks, 3 steel yoke knot passing pulleys, 90 feet of $3/4$ inch carrier rope, and 35 feet of $1/4$ inch manila check rope."[2]

Not only did the Louden hay carrier make unloading hay much easier, the invention encouraged farmers to build taller and longer barns because the hay could be moved much more easily.

NOTES

1. Allen G. Noble and Hubert G. H. Wilhelm, eds., *Barns in the Midwest* (Athens, OH: Ohio University Press, 1995), 87–90.

2. Sears, Roebuck and Co., 1908 Catalog, 481.

In those days the typical midwestern dairy barn housed cattle on the lower level and provided space for hay storage on the upper level. The storage areas, called haymows, were located on either side of the driveway area in the barn, which often was called a threshing floor—language left over from the days when farmers threshed their grain in the barn with flails. Pa slowly guided the wagon load of hay into the barn, the hayrack creaking and the barn's floorboards protesting. In 1946 we had installed a hay carrier along the uppermost part of our new barn, running from one end to the other. (In the old barn we pitched the hay off the hay wagon by hand.) The carrier consisted of a track, which ran just under the highest part of the roof from one end of the barn to the other, and a series of ropes and pulleys fastened to a double-harpoon hayfork, made of two thirty-inch tines sixteen inches apart. Each tine included a little built-in finger that opened and closed and kept the hay in place until it was released with a trip rope.

It was my job to push the harpoon fork into the load of hay and activate the little lever that opened the fingers. Meanwhile, Pa unhitched Frank from the wagon and led him outdoors, where he hitched him to the end of the long, three-quarter-inch-thick hayfork rope. With the harpoon fork in place, I yelled to Darrel and Don, who were driving the horse on the hayfork rope. I heard one of them say, "Giddy up." The rope tightened, the pulleys squeaked, and a huge bunch of hay began slowly lifting from the wagon. I held a quarter-inch rope tied to the trip mechanism. The rope slowly ran through my fingers as the bunch of hay moved upward to the hayfork track. Pa waited in the haymow, where he would fork the hay into all the corners.

When the fork load of hay reached the track in the top of the barn, the mechanism engaged and the hay began moving along the track over the haymow where Pa waited. When the hay was right where he wanted it, he yelled, "Trip it!" I yanked on the trip rope, and the load of hay fell into the haymow with a swoosh and a swirl of dust and hay leaves. At the same time I yelled, "Whoa," to my brothers, who were driving Frank on the hayfork rope. If the horse kept going, the hayfork mechanism would reach the end of the barn and pull down the entire hay-carrier system. Stopping on time was critical.

With the hayfork tripped, my brothers turned Frank around and drove him back to the barn to repeat the process. With the trip rope, I pulled the harpoon fork back to where I could push it once more into the hay still on the wagon. We would repeat the process until all the hay was off the wagon.

Meanwhile, Pa kept forking hay into all corners of the haymow to make sure we could store as much hay as possible. His job was the hottest, most miserable of all the tasks associated with unloading the wagon. It could be eighty-five degrees outside, and under the

HAY PRESSES (BALERS)

The hay balers I knew were portable, meaning a tractor pulled them around the field as they worked. Early hay balers, called hay presses, had been in existence since the mid-1800s. H. L. Emery of Albany, New York, manufactured one of the early models in 1853. He claimed he could bale five 250-pound bales in an hour with his machine. The bales were two feet by two feet by four feet long. Another inventor, George Ertel of Quincy, Illinois, began manufacturing hay presses in 1866. Two horses walking in a circle powered this hay press through an elaborate gear system.[1]

Many other manufacturers made hay presses. R. K. Dederick & Sons advertised its press this way: "Three-fourths of all the hay-presses in use are Dederick's. All the best hay shippers and farmers

An early hay press. Loose hay was fed into the chute on top of the machine and was pressed into bales. (PHOTO BY STEVE APPS, TAKEN AT STONEFIELD HISTORIC SITE)

use them. World's fair prizes . . . puts from 10 to 12 tons in a car. Requires less money."[2]

Farmers hauled their loose hay to the hay press, which was powered by a horse-powered sweep, an elaborate mechanism of gears and poles to which as many as six horses were hitched. The horses walked in a circle and thus turned horse power into mechanical power that fueled the machine. (For more on sweeps, see page 143.)

This circa 1917 International Harvester catalog advertised the company's hay presses. (WHI IMAGE ID 22732)

NOTES

1. J. Brownlee Davidson and Leon Wilson Chase, *Farm Machinery: Practical Hints for Handy-men* (Guilford, CT: The Lyons Press, 1999), 187–188; Ronald Stokes Barlow, *300 Years of Farm Implements and Machinery, 1630–1930* (Iola, WI: Krause Publications, 2003), 68–69.

2. *Farm Journal*, August 1898, 192.

barn roof the temperature by mid-afternoon would climb to more than one hundred degrees. Hay leaves and dust flew everywhere with each load of hay dumped into the mow.

When all the hay was unloaded, we hitched Frank back to the wagon along with Charlie and returned to the hay field to make another load. One load after the other, from morning until late in the afternoon, if the weather held. Pa followed closely the old saying, "Make hay while the sun shines." In about three weeks the haying season would end, and we would move on to the next cycle of summer farmwork.

Some farmers made enough hay so they had extra to sell. The hay was generally shipped via railcars. Prior to loading, the hay was pressed into bales, which allowed a considerably greater weight of hay to be packed into each car. These early hay presses were stationary and powered by horses. By the mid-1940s portable hay balers pulled by a tractor essentially replaced the stationary hay presses.

After World War II tractors began replacing horses on many midwestern farms. With tractors came portable hay balers, which eliminated several old haymaking tasks: bunching hay, hauling loose hay to the barn, and unloading loose hay into the haymow. A tractor-pulled hay baler followed the side-delivery rake's rope of hay, gathered it up, and pressed it into one-hundred-pound wire-tied blocks, which we loaded on wagons and stacked in the barn.

When tractors and portable hay balers arrived, hay making with horses disappeared. The slow and deliberate pace set by a team of horses was replaced by the tractor and rubber-tired hay wagon speeding down the road to the hay field and hurrying back with a load of hay bales. To be sure, making hay with horses was dusty, dirty, difficult work. But it had its pleasurable moments. It was a quiet task—no roaring engines and no stink of exhaust fumes mixing with the smell of new-mown hay. We could hear songbirds and watch hawks soaring in cloudless skies. And we admired the beauty of a field of mown hay, the bunches marching up and down the hills and filling the valleys. Riding on the top of a load of loose hay pulled by the team moving slowly across the hay field, onto the gravel road, into our driveway, and to the barn provided a much-needed rest and a chance to appreciate the summer days. It seemed there was always a breeze when riding high up on a load of hay, so it was cooler there—not a bad way to spend the hottest weeks of a midwestern summer.

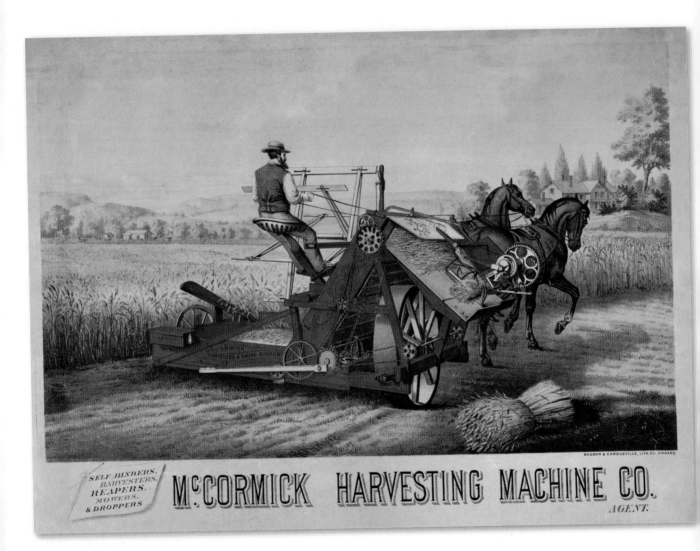

Circa 1882 McCormick grain binder poster (WHI IMAGE ID 3600)

EARLY HARVEST

Haying season stretched into late July. When it was over we usually had a week or two to catch up on overlooked projects before it was time to begin harvesting. With a herd of fifteen or twenty cattle plus three horses out on pasture the entire summer, the fences always needed attention. If the cows got out, usually into a neighbor's cornfield, Pa would take emergency action to repair the fence, which meant a temporary fix until we had more time.

Fixing a fence usually involved setting new fence posts, stringing barbed wire, and cutting any tree limbs that hung over the fence wires. Pa never replaced anything until it broke. With fence posts this meant the posts stayed in place until they fell over or were smashed over because a tree limb had fallen on the fence wire. He bought new cedar fence posts, eight feet long and six or eight inches in diameter, and stored them in a pile behind the wagon shed. Cedar trees did not grow on our farm, or in the area, so they had to be hauled in from northern Wisconsin. Cedar resisted rot more than other available wood—a post could stand for up to twenty years, sometimes more. (Of course, these were the days before treated lumber.)

On a dewy morning in late July, Pa would hitch Frank and Charlie to the hay wagon. We'd toss on a few cedar posts, the hand-operated posthole digger, a shovel, a crowbar, a roll of barbed wire Pa had purchased from the Wild Rose Cooperative farm supply store, a hammer or two, some staples, and the water jug, and we were off. Without fail the fence in need of repair was in the far corner of the farm, sometimes more than half a mile from the farmstead. So we'd bounce along the cow lane to the back pasture and spend the morning digging postholes, setting posts, stringing wire, stretching the wire tight, and nailing it to the new posts. There often weren't enough leather gloves to go around, so wire cuts were common.

The most difficult task of fence making was digging the postholes. The hole digger worked well, until you struck a stone—the chances of which were nearly 100 percent on our farm. Pa was a stickler for setting the fence posts in an absolutely straight row. This meant digging with the shovel and using the crowbar to remove the stone. Of course, when you first hit the stone with the posthole digger, you had no idea how big it was—the size of your fist, or the size of a horse? We determined the size of the stone through sheer brute effort, digging with the shovel and probing with the crowbar. If the stone was too large to move, we'd move down the line a few feet and start a new hole.

When fence work was finished, we returned to hoeing. In fact, when Pa couldn't think of anything else that needed doing, we hoed. We hoed potatoes and corn, cucumbers and green beans. We hoed in the hollows to challenge the quack grass—though we never killed it. We hoed out ragweeds and lamb's-quarter, the bull thistles in the valleys and the purslane on the side hills. Pa was constantly instructing us about which weed was which and how to best attack it with the hoe. "Cut off the weeds, don't bury them," was his mantra. Of course, it was easier to pile a little dirt on a weed than to chop it off.

To his credit, he always hoed with us. To our unhappiness, that meant there was no goofing off, no cutting corners, always quality hoeing. About mid-afternoon, while hoeing quack grass in a cornfield's hollows, I often thought I'd rather be making fence, even when it meant wrestling with stones as large as horses.

Some machinery manufacturers advertised equipment to replace hoes. "Hallock's Success Anti-Clog Weeder" was one. This weeder removed weeds with its "flat teeth—twice as flexible, durable and effective as round teeth." But the machine removed the crop as well. No weeds, no crop—a clean field.[1]

No matter what field work we were doing, Pa, my brothers, and I did the barn chores each morning and evening. In summer the cows were on pasture, so the barn chores were relatively simple, with no manure handling involved. Our chores included feeding and grooming the horses, mucking out their stalls, fetching the cows from the pasture, feeding them some ground feed supplement, milking them, and turning them back out to pasture. We could do all of this in less than a couple hours, so we had plenty of time to devote to the summer's field work.

Summer days were long: daylight by five-thirty and darkness holding off until nine (there was no daylight saving time in those days). Except for the time spent at our three meals, we worked every one of those hours from daylight to dark, falling into bed shortly after nine exhausted, and stumbling out to the barn the following morning, sleep still in our eyes. We did take off a couple hours to attend the free outdoor movies in Wild Rose on Tuesday evenings and another few hours for a trip to town on Saturday night. Sunday was a day of rest—well, mostly. We still had to do the barn chores Sunday morning and evening, but the rest of the day my brothers and I were free to go fishing, swimming, hiking in the woods, or visiting the neighbor boys. Most Sundays we attended church, an activity as required as hoeing potatoes.

The Pranica family harvests cucumbers in Sobieski, Wisconsin, circa 1941. Cukes were a common cash crop in the sand country of central and northeastern Wisconsin. Even today most cucumbers are handpicked.

(WHI IMAGE ID 38714)

Harvesting Cash Crops

In mid- to late July, the cucumber and bean growers began harvesting their crops. Both required hand picking (today beans are harvested with huge machines; cucumbers still require hand picking). Picking cucumbers and beans was a family operation from which only the very youngest members were excused. With warm weather and regular rains, cucumbers required picking about every third day for six weeks or so. Farmers picked green beans about once a week.

The farmer and farm family hauled the beans and cucumbers to buying stations, where they immediately received payment for their product. In central Wisconsin nearly every village had green bean and cucumber receiving stations, so few farmers had to travel more than five miles to make a delivery. Receiving stations bought green beans by the pound. Cucumber receiving stations sorted the cucumbers into grades from grade 1 (the smallest) to grade 5 (those as large as your wrist). Farmers were paid by the pound, according to grade, with the smallest cucumbers—gherkins—receiving the highest payment. For both cucumbers and green beans, Pa let us keep the full amount earned for what we picked. Some days we might earn ten dollars for picking these cash crops, a far cry from the one dollar earned in a full day of backbreaking potato picking. Picking the summer crops was often more pleasant, too—warmer (maybe too warm) than the frosty October mornings when we shivered our way down the potato row.

We harvested cucumbers and green beans starting in mid-July and continuing on until frost killed the plants, usually in mid-September at our central Wisconsin location.

Tobacco harvesting began in late August or early September. The tobacco growers walked down the rows chopping off the near-head-high tobacco plants, using an ax made by the blacksmith from a carpenter's handsaw, sharpened to an edge and with a handle attached. A skilled person could chop a tobacco plant with one blow.

The plants were left to wilt in the sun for a couple of hours and then attached to wooden laths in a process called spearing. Workers loaded the laths of speared tobacco onto a rack on a horse-drawn wagon. The teamster hauled the load to a tobacco shed,

Harvesting tobacco was hard labor. Here the tobacco plants have already been cut; in the background a team hauls the "speared" tobacco to the tobacco barn for drying. (WHI IMAGE ID 30171)

POTATO DIGGERS

Several machinery manufacturers advertised their potato diggers with exaggeration and flair. D. Y. Hallock & Son of York, Pennsylvania, said this about its machine, which looked like a modified walking plow: "Does the work ten men would do with forks. It's a money maker to work with, to hire out, or to sell by taking an agency. Nothing ever offered to farmers ever had such a boom. Hallocks' Success Gilt Edge Potato Harvester."

The Hoover, Prout Company of Avery, Ohio, manufactured a horse-drawn potato digger that allowed the operator to ride. The ad simply said, "The Hoover Digger digs potatoes rapidly, clean and cheap." The Dowden Company of Prairie City, Iowa, asked, "How many potatoes did you plant? If you have an acre you cannot afford to dig them by hand. The Dowden Potato digger digs potatoes better, cleaner and cheaper than can be done by hand."[1]

Three horses pull a potato digger, 1928. Once the potatoes were dug, they still had to be handpicked and hauled from the field to storage cellars. (WHI IMAGE ID 41604)

NOTES

1. *Farm Journal*, August 1898, 182, 184.

where the laths were hung on long poles. The tobacco was left to air dry, which took two to three months, until sometime in December.[2]

As with tobacco farming, nearly every aspect of harvesting potatoes was hand labor. By the 1930s horse-drawn mechanical potato diggers were available, but they were cumbersome, hard-pulling machines that did not work well in stony potato fields. A horse-drawn potato digger consisted of a blade that dug into the ground beneath the potato hills. The potatoes came out of the ground onto a heavy endless steel chain and fell on the ground behind the machine so they could be picked by hand. We had one, but we never used it. Frank and Charlie could hardly pull it, especially up hills, and our stony farm provided more of a challenge than the machine was designed to handle.

We harvested potatoes after we filled the silo and before we harvested ripe corn. Our country school closed for two weeks of "potato vacation," usually in early October. Pa, often with the help of a hired man, dug the potatoes by hand using a six-tine barn fork. Each man dug two rows at a time, backing his way across the potato field, which in some years was twenty acres. The pickers, my brothers and I, picked the dug-up potatoes by hand, tossed them into buckets, and then dumped the filled buckets into wooden bushel potato crates. At noon and again in late afternoon, Pa steered Frank and Charlie alongside the filled potato boxes, hoisted the boxes onto the steel-wheeled wagon, and hauled them to the house. There we dumped them into potato bins in the cellar under the house or into bins in the potato cellar, a little building built into a side hill just west of the chicken house. Its bins held several hundred bushels of potatoes, which would remain there until midwinter, when the price of potatoes went up and Pa sold them (see page 172).

Harvesting Grain

By mid-July the oat heads had begun turning from green to golden brown. Pa, Don, Darrel, and I walked to the oat field at least twice a week to check the crop. The oats on top of the hills matured more quickly than oats growing in the valleys where the soil was heavier, particularly in seasons when we didn't have sufficient rain. Hot, sunny days also speeded up maturity.

Some years we'd grow a few acres of winter wheat or winter rye in addition to our twenty or thirty acres of oats. Both wheat and rye were planted in fall and ripened before the oats did.

In late July Pa would announce at the breakfast table: "It's time to clean up the grain binder." Pa housed the binder, a McCormick-Deering, in a machine shed. After a year of storage, dust and bird droppings covered the machine. Pa hitched the team to the binder, one of the largest and most complicated mechanical devices on the farm, and hauled it out of the shed, and we spent several days greasing, cleaning, and repairing it. Then we retrieved three long, slatted canvases from their storage place upstairs in the house, where mice were less likely to find them. We fastened the canvases over the rollers, and we were ready to cut grain.

A grain binder was a complex machine. A typical binder consisted of a large metal drive wheel, referred to as a bull wheel; a sickle bar for cutting the grain (similar to that used on hay mowers); a wooden reel with four to six slats that pushed the standing grain against the sickle bar; slatted canvases to move the cut grain to the binding mechanism; a knotting mechanism, which formed the cut grain into a bundle, wrapped a length of binding twine around it, tied a knot, and ejected the bundle; and a bundle carrier to gather the bundles so several could be collected and dropped at one time.

Much could—and did—go wrong with a grain binder. The sickle bar might strike a stone and be broken, the slatted canvas might get caught and tear, or the knotting mechanism might fail. The latter was one of the most common problems, and when the knotter failed, the binder tossed out loose bundles. But it seemed no matter how well the grain binder worked, it always tossed a few loose bundles. A person shocking grain always carried a few lengths of binder twine to tie the loose bundles by hand.

With the binder in good order (or the best we could make it, as it was old and had cut many acres), Pa headed for the oat field. Frank and Charlie had grown a little soft since the haying season, so they were in high spirits as Pa lowered the sickle bar and the binder began its tour around the outside of the field. The first swath cut was always the most difficult, as there was a wire fence and stone piles to contend with. With the first cut made, the task was easier.

This style of McCormick twine-tie grain binder was first built in 1883. McCormick built its first twine binder in 1881 and continually made improvements to lighten the machine and make it more durable.

(WHI IMAGE ID 22888)

REAPERS

When humankind first began growing and harvesting grain, people seeded and harvested the crop by hand. For many years the human harvesters used sickles to cut the grain. A sickle had a short handle with a curved blade, and the operator had to bend over to use it. Once the grain was cut, the farmer (or more likely his wife and children) bound it by hand into bundles or sheaves. On a good day, a farmer could cut an acre of grain with a sickle.

By the early 1800s the cradle had replaced the sickle as the implement of choice for cutting grain. The cradle was a large scythe with wooden fingers above it that held the grain until it was laid in rows on the back stroke. The cradle cut a deeper and a wider swath than a sickle. What's more, the operator could stand upright rather than working in a squatting position. Using a cradle, two men—one cradling and the other gathering and

Illustrations in an 1883 McCormick Harvesting Machine Company catalog portrayed "The Evolution of the Reaper." (WHI IMAGE ID 36161 AND 36163)

REAPERS

binding—could harvest and shock two or more acres a day.

But the work was still slow and tedious, especially for farmers who moved into the midwestern states in the middle 1800s and began growing dozens of acres of wheat. Some farmers planted more than a hundred acres of wheat, which required a substantial number of cradlers and gatherers to harvest the crop.

An early settler in Sauk County, Wisconsin, William Toole, reminisced about his early farming experiences in a series of articles published by a local newspaper. He wrote, "For the first few years our grain was all cut with a cradle . . . with the old-fashioned scythe. If there was a reaper or mower anywhere in Excelsior [where he settled] or joining towns previous of 1865 or 1866, I did not know of it. Our first machine mowing was done by a neighbor who had purchased a Manny reaper. Removing the platform, and putting in a smooth sickle, changed the reaper to a mower."[1]

In the early 1800s several English inventors experimented with mechanical grain harvesters, or reapers, as they were called. In 1806 a Mr. Gladstone invented a machine with a revolving cutter and the horse walking to the side—the introduction of the side cut. The grain fell on a platform, where a man removed it with a hand rake. But in their 1908 work *Farm Machinery: Practical Hints for Handy-men*, authors Davidson and Chase wrote, "As a whole, this machine was not successful."[2]

Several U.S. inventors developed versions of the reaper in the early 1800s. Obed Hussey of Baltimore received a patent December 31, 1833, for quite an

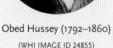

Obed Hussey (1792–1860)
(WHI IMAGE ID 24855)

Cyrus McCormick (1809–1884)
(WHI IMAGE ID 8363)

advanced reaper. It was pulled by two horses and cut grain with a cutter attached to a pitman, which operated from a crank geared to the main axle of the machine. The pitman moved the cutter back and forth, shearing off the grain, which fell onto a little platform. Some version of Hussey's pitman and sickle bar cutter became a part of almost every reaper design that followed.

When Cyrus McCormick of Virginia learned of Hussey's machine and its patent, he quickly filed for a patent on his reaper and received it June 21, 1834, six months after Hussey. McCormick said his machine had been built and used before Hussey's and claimed his patent should be given preference. Several years of "patent wars" between Hussey and McCormick followed. Eventually Hussey lost out to McCormick, a superior businessman.[3]

McCormick's 1834 machine included a revolving reel with wooden slats that pushed the standing

(continued on next page)

REAPERS

(continued from page 135)

grain against the cutting knives.[4] McCormick continued making improvements on his machine, including adding a mechanism for raising and lowering the reel.

With McCormick's reaper, eight men and two horses could harvest ten acres of wheat a day, which was little different from what a similar number of men swinging a cradle could do.[5] But with a reaper, horses could replace some of the human power, a long-sought goal of most farmers. In his book on the history of Wisconsin agriculture, Joseph Schafer wrote about a Dane County farmer who grew eight hundred acres of wheat in 1860, yielding twenty-five thousand bushels, or about thirty-one bushels per acre. The farm, owned by a Mr. DeForest, employed eight reaping machines and about sixty men for the harvest. Schafer surmised the reapers were of the type that required two men to operate, one driving the team and the other hand raking the cut wheat from the machine. Five men followed each machine, tying the wheat stalks into bundles and making grain shocks.[6]

In 1847 Cyrus McCormick moved his operations to Chicago. By this time his two brothers, William S. McCormick and Leander J. McCormick, worked with him. But Cyrus was in charge. He was a superior salesman, traveling far and wide proclaiming the virtues of his reaper and conducting demonstrations of its use. He won awards at international shows and accumulated acclaim for his invention. Meanwhile, Leander supervised the Chicago manufacturing plant, constantly improving on the machine. William

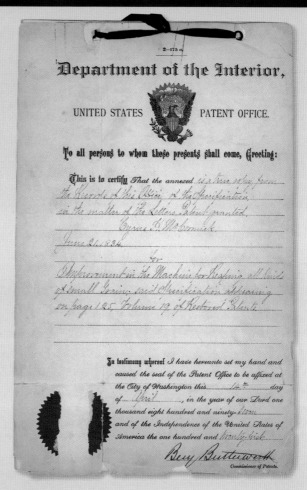

An excerpt from the patent for Cyrus McCormick's reaper, June 21, 1834 (WHI IMAGE ID 2426)

supervised the sales department and supply purchasing and oversaw bill collections—a constant problem, as many farmers were eager to purchase but slow in paying.[7]

Probably the greatest boon to reaper sales was the Civil War. As thousands of men left their farms

REAPERS

to fight, they left behind thousands of acres of grain to be harvested. Those boys, older men, and women left behind simply were unable to harvest the thousands of wheat acres with cradles, as men had done for years. Many turned to McCormick's reaper.

By the mid-1850s the McCormick Company employed 250 workers and was producing more than 2,500 reapers a year. When the company's factory burned in the 1871 Chicago fire, it built a larger factory along the south branch of the Chicago River. It soon employed about eight hundred men.[8]

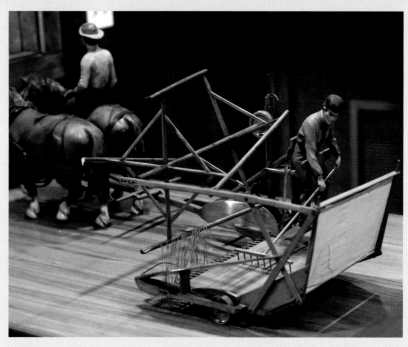

A salesmen's model of Cyrus McCormick's first reaper, which replaced the backbreaking cradle and sickle for cutting grain. (PHOTO BY STEVE APPS, TAKEN AT STONEFIELD HISTORIC SITE)

Binding the grain after the reaper cut it remained an onerous task, requiring workers to follow the machine and tie the cut grain into bundles. The Marsh Harvester, invented by Charles and William Marsh of Dekalb, Illinois, in 1857, made the task somewhat easier. After the Marsh Harvester cut the grain, a canvas belt moved it to a little platform where two people could sit and tie the grain into bundles as the machine moved through the field.[9] The Marshes partnered with John Hollister of Plano, Illinois, and were soon selling their harvester worldwide. They claimed their harvester would cut an acre of grain in less than an hour.[10]

William Deering, born in Maine, was another important figure in the reaper manufacturing business. An industrialist who made his fortune working in his father's woolen mill, Deering moved to Illinois in 1873 with the intention of buying farmland. While there he visited his old friend Elijah Gammon, who had recently acquired the rights to the Marsh Harvester. Gammon convinced Deering that there was money to be made in the reaper business. Deering invested forty thousand dollars in the Marsh Harvester enterprise; a couple years later, when Gammon became ill, Deering took over the business.

(continued on next page)

REAPERS

(continued from page 137)

The Marsh Harvester provided a platform where a person could ride and tie the grain into bundles by hand.
(PHOTO BY STEVE APPS, TAKEN AT STONEFIELD HISTORIC SITE)

Deering bought out Gammon in 1875 and the business took off, eventually rivaling McCormick in sales. Deering moved his operations to Chicago in 1880. The factory was soon building six thousand harvesters a year.[11]

NOTES

1. William Toole, "As to Reaping Grain," *Sauk County Farmer* (Baraboo, WI), April 1917.

2. J. Brownlee Davidson and Leon Wilson Chase, *Farm Machinery: Practical Hints for Handy-men* (Guilford, CT: The Lyons Press, 1999), 138.

3. William T. Hutchinson, *Cyrus Hall McCormick: Seed-Time, 1809–1856* (New York: The Century Company, 1930), 75–82.

4. Davidson and Chase, *Farm Machinery*, 139–141.

5. R. Carlyle Buley, *The Old Northwest Pioneer Period: 1815–1840* (Bloomington: Indiana University Press, 1951), 178, 180.

6. Joseph Schafer, *A History of Agriculture in Wisconsin* (Madison: State Historical Society of Wisconsin, 1922), 88.

7. Hutchinson, *Cyrus Hall McCormick*, 99–101.

8. Mark R. Wilson, "Dictionary of Leading Chicago Businesses (1820–2000)," *The Electronic Encyclopedia of Chicago* (Chicago: Chicago Historical Society, 2005).

9. Craig Canine, *Dream Reaper* (Chicago: University of Chicago Press, 1995), 46–47.

10. Illinois Historical Digitization Project, "Marsh Harvester," www.dig.lib.niu.edu/dekalb/hist-marsh.html.

11. Canine, *Dream Reaper*, 47.

BINDERS

One important feature differentiates a reaper from a grain binder: a grain binder not only cuts grain, it also binds it into bundles. And the grain binder does this with a mechanical knotter, one of the cleverest inventions known.

It seemed an impossible task to mimic what human fingers do when they tie a knot. But on July 22, 1850, Ohio inventor John Heath became the first person to design a machine that automatically pressed wheat stalks together, wrapped a twine around them, and cut the twine to the correct length. (A person still had to tie the knot, however.)

One serious problem for knot binder inventors was finding suitable binding material. Traditionally straw had been used, but it was not strong enough for the mechanical process.

In 1856 C. A. McPhitridge from Missouri designed a device for tying wire around a grain bundle. A simple twist with the fingers would fasten the loose ends of wire together.[1]

Wire-tie binders quickly became popular. The McCormick factory began making them, as did other former reaper manufacturers, but it was the wire itself that led to the demise of the wire-tie machines. Farmers said their cows were dying after eating pieces of wire. The milling industry complained loudly. The *St. Paul Pioneer Press* in 1878 carried this editorial:

(continued on next page)

A woman sits on a horse-drawn McCormick grain binder, circa 1900. This obviously is a posed photo, as the woman's wardrobe is ill-suited to the dusty, dirty work of driving a team on a grain binder. (WHI IMAGE ID 9515)

BINDERS

(continued from page 139)

There's a bad thing brewing for the farmers who used the self-binders with wire to bind their grain. The Minneapolis millers sound the keynote of warning, having had a meeting to compare notes on the wire as regard damage done to bolt cloth and mill stones. Mr. Stokes of the Banner Mill showed us pieces of wire taken from their burrs, although he was unaware that any wheat had been purchased which was bound with wire.

Mr. Wise, of the Mankato Review, has investigated at the Mankato mills, and learns that utmost caution is being used by the millers there to prevent wire reaching the stones, by putting it through extra screens. The case is a serious one and every farmer who uses wire for binding should see to it that the bands are removed when threshing, else the price of wheat may be materially reduced.[2]

Even if no damage was done to miller's machinery, the question of feed alone would be sufficient to make millers shy of wheat bound with wire.

Meanwhile, a young man who had moved to Wisconsin from New York in 1845 invented a knotting device that one day would be found on nearly all grain binders. But for years no one paid any attention to John Francis Appleby's invention, seeing it merely as a curiosity.

When Appleby returned from fighting in the Civil War, he settled near Mazomanie, where he unsuccessfully tested his first grain binder. In the early 1870s he moved to Beloit, where he worked with machinery manufacturers Gustavus Stone and Charles H. Parker. By 1874 Appleby had developed a successful wire-tie binder, but he faced the growing refusal of farmers to use wire. Still he worked at perfecting a twine binder and received patents in 1878 and 1879.[3]

On this circa 1883 Deering all-steel grain binder poster, the old-timers in the foreground are discussing how "harvest isn't what it used to be." (WHI IMAGE ID 4386)

BINDERS

Parker and Stone Manufacturers produced the first binders using Appleby's knotter and twine. The company shipped several railcar loads of twine binders throughout the country.[4] Farmers quickly accepted this new machine as an alternative to the wire-tie binders. William Ellis, a Minnesota farmer, wrote to the company in February 1879:

> I purchased of your agent last year an Appleby twine binder. In its behalf I want to say, first, that I went to see the Wood Lock, the McCormick Automatic and the Marsh wire binders and am satisfied that I got the best binder on the market: second, that I cut through spots where I had to drive through on a trot to keep the machine in motion (the ground was so wet) and the binder did its work well: third, that it makes a bundle for shocking and stacking that beats all the wire binders and hand ties that I have seen, and, last, that I would rather thresh the grain bound by your machine than all the wire and hand binding that I have threshed, and I have run a machine the last five falls. I would not give my machine for any other in the market.[5]

William Deering, an astute businessman, struck an agreement with Appleby to use his knotter on a Deering grain binder. In 1880 Deering secretly manufactured three thousand twine binders with Appleby's knotter. They sold immediately.[6] The era of wire-tie binders was over. (Interestingly, some years later hay balers would experience a similar metamorphosis from wire- to twine-bound bales.)

The Deering Harvester Company flourished, boasting more employees than McCormick by the late 1880s. In 1902 McCormick, Deering, the Plano Manufacturing Company, and two smaller firms merged to form International Harvester. By 1910 International Harvester employed seventeen thousand workers in the Chicago area and was one of the leading industrial corporations in the United States.[7]

Several other machinery manufacturers got into the grain binder business, including John Deere, J. I. Case, and Massey Harris. Grain binders continued to be used well into the mid-1900s and disappeared only when tractors took over from horses and grain combines arrived, taking care of both cutting and threshing all in one trip across the field.

NOTES

1. Craig Canine, *Dream Reaper* (Chicago: University of Chicago Press, 1995), 48.

2. *St. Paul Pioneer Press*, October 19, 1878.

3. Dictionary of Wisconsin History, Wisconsin Historical Society, "Appleby, John Francis, 1840–1917," www.wisconsinhistory.org/dictionary.

4. "Beloit to Honor Inventor of First Twine Binder," *Beloit Daily News*, June 1, 1911.

5. Ibid.

6. Canine, *Dream Reaper*, 51.

7. "International Harvester Co.," *Encyclopedia of Chicago: Electronic Encyclopedia of Chicago* (Chicago: Chicago Historical Society, 2005).

Pa sat high up on the binder seat where he could oversee all the operations and handle the team. The sickle bar chattered as the binder moved slowly along. The machine did not pull easily, and going up hills challenged the two-horse team. The reel turned slowly, pushing the golden grain stalks into the sickle. The slatted canvases pulled the cut grain into the machine on their way to the knotter. After every few feet, the knotter arms turned and a freshly tied bundle bounced onto the metal carrier, which consisted of several metal fingers each about three feet long. By pushing a foot lever, Pa collapsed the carrier, dumping the collected grain bundles on the ground.

My brothers and I sat waiting for Pa to make several passes around the field before we began standing the oat bundles into grain shocks. As with everything else on the farm, there is a right way and a wrong way to build a grain shock. The right way required grabbing a bundle under each arm, putting forward a bent knee, and then standing a bundle on each side of your knee with the tops of the bundles (where the oat heads were) touching. You added bundles on each side of the center pair until you had a total of ten bundles. The idea was for air to move freely through the shock so as to dry the grain.

Shocking grain was hot, backbreaking work. You had to bend over and thrust a knee forward with every pair of bundles. There was no cheating, no shortcuts. You did it right, or the shock fell over and you had to do it again. Of course, Pa not only watched the binder and the team, he had his eye on us as well, making sure each grain shock was as perfect as perfect could be. We boys followed behind the binder, constructing shock after shock, until we got to one of the hollows, where the grain was taller and the bundles heavier. Bull thistles grew in the hollows, and no matter how heavy your shirt, the thistle spines stuck you in the arms, adding further misery to the work.

By midmorning the novelty of this new job had completely worn off. My brothers and I suggested that hoeing might be easier than grain shocking; at least when you were hoeing, no bull thistle spines stuck you in the arms. We even agreed that grain shocking was considerably more difficult than bunching hay. When bunching hay we got to use a three-tine

An 1885 William Deering catalog featured the company's horse-drawn grain binder.

(WHI IMAGE ID 39516)

fork, but there were no mechanical devices for when shocking grain. Your hands, arms, and back became the tools.

At day's end, when the field had been cut and all the bundles stood in shocks, Pa once more took time to survey the work we'd done. A field of grain shocks, golden yellow against a clear blue sky, is a thing of beauty, a piece of rural art. I didn't appreciate it at the time; my sore back and scratched arms were of greater concern.

Pa didn't want the shocked grain to stand and dry in the field for more than a week—the chances of it getting rained on were just too great. The next step in the harvesting process was threshing the grain, one of the most important activities of the year for many farmers.

Threshing Grain

By the late 1800s steam engine tractors had replaced horse sweeps as the main source of threshing power. These monster tractors pulled the threshing machines from farm to farm during the threshing season. Generally, one farmer owned both tractor and threshing machine and moved from one rural community to another, first threshing his neighbors and then moving on. A device on the thresher recorded the number of bushels threshed, and farmers paid the machine's owner for each bushel. A group of neighbors moved along with the thresher from farm to farm to help with the work.

Milton Vroman, who farmed several miles west of my home farm, owned a threshing machine and did custom work. He brought his machine, powered by a John Deere R tractor, into our neighborhood each threshing season. The tractor had a two-cylinder diesel engine and was first made by Deere in 1949. The tractor's big engine kicked out nearly fifty horsepower and was started with a smaller built-in gasoline engine. The R made a wonderful sound, a deep-throated "pom, pom, pom."

The earliest threshing machines, though, were powered by horses walking in a circle, their work transferred through a series of gears to the thresher. Then, from the late 1800s to the 1940s, monstrous steam engines powered threshing machines. Coal and/or wood fueled the big steam engines, which were very similar to the steam locomotives that pulled trains. When gasoline and diesel tractors started arriving on farms in the 1920s and 1930s, they were lacking the sound of the steam whistle, a feature of all steam engines. As a kid, the steam whistle is what I enjoyed most about steam engines. There was no sound like it. It could be heard for miles, especially on still days, when it seemed to hang in the air like the call of wild geese winging south in fall.

HORSEPOWER SWEEPS AND TREADMILLS

The horse-powered treadmill was an early way of turning animal power into mechanical power. As the horses walked "uphill," they moved an apron that was attached to a series of gears and pulleys that powered everything from small threshing machines, like this one at Old World Wisconsin historic site, to corn shellers and other farm equipment. (WISCONSIN HISTORICAL SOCIETY PHOTO © LOYD HEATH)

As large new machines such as hay presses, ensilage cutters, and threshing machines came on the market, inventors searched for ways to power them. Several early inventors developed machines that converted animal power to machine power. One of the simplest was a treadmill. An animal—goat, dog, pony, horse, ox—walked on an inclined ramp, which moved as the animal walked. The earliest treadmills powered butter churns, corn shellers, washing machines, and water pumps. Larger treadmills, some using two or even three horses, powered larger machines, such as sawmills. But the treadmill could not provide sufficient power for large threshing machines and hay presses.

By the middle 1800s some farmers were using horse-powered sweeps. With a sweep, several horses walked in a circle on the ground, hitched to poles that were attached to a central hub. Through a

HORSEPOWER SWEEPS AND TREADMILLS

Horses provide power to a thresher via a horsepower sweep, circa 1900. (WHI IMAGE ID 31821)

series of gears, the animal power was transferred to the machine it was powering. The gears were arranged so the power of the horses could be speeded up, as threshing machines required both speed and power. Some of the larger sweeps accommodated as many as six teams, or twelve horses. The operator of the horse-powered sweep stood in the center of the walking teams, keeping them moving at a steady pace.

In 1893 Heebner and Company of Lansdale, Pennsylvania, offered a treadmill for one, two, or three horses.[1] The Appleton Manufacturing Company in Batavia, Illinois, advertised a "Success One Horse Tread Power. For running cream separators, churns, pumps, small grinding mill, feed cutter or any machine because the largest horse can work it with ease."[2]

By the late 1800s, steam engines and steam-powered tractors became available, replacing the

horse sweep, especially for the powering of the big threshing machines.[3]

NOTES

1. *Farm Journal*, March 1893, 74.

2. *Farm Journal*, June 1898, 153.

3. Ronald Stokes Barlow, *300 Years of Farm Implements and Machinery: 1630–1930* (Iola, WI: Krause Publications, 2003), 188–189; Paul C. Johnson, *Farm Power in the Making of America* (Des Moines, IA: Wallace-Homestead Book Company, 1978), 14–21.

Threshing was a community activity, with neighbors helping neighbors as the threshing machine moved from farm to farm.
(WHI IMAGE ID 53677)

Threshers, sometimes called separators, were huge machines—the largest implement we ever used at our farm. These machines stood eight to ten feet high and as much as thirty feet long. The machine threshed the grain and separated the grain kernels from the straw and chaff. The threshed grain rattled down a metal chute to which grain bags were attached. A blower shot the straw and chaff out a movable pipe into a straw stack.

Threshing involved the entire neighborhood. Early on threshing day, neighbors began arriving at our farm. Pa asked three neighbors to bring their teams and wagons; he asked three or four more to "carry," which meant toting on their shoulders bags filled with oats from the threshing machine to the grain bins in the granary. Additionally, he invited two neighbors to be "field pitchers," helping to load the bundle wagons. Someone usually volunteered to operate the straw blower, a dusty, dirty, but necessary job.

Cooking for a hungry crew of threshers was no small task. There was also a friendly competition among neighbor women as to who could cook the most memorable meals. Ma asked her sister, Louise, to help with the cooking and serving, and usually one or more neighbor women volunteered to help as well.

For those of us who traveled from farm to farm in the neighborhood as part of the threshing crew, the meals were the highlight of the threshing season. And such meals they were: usually two kinds of meat—roast beef, pork chops—mounds of mashed potatoes, bowls of thick brown gravy, carrots and peas, thickly sliced homemade bread with fresh butter. The desserts for the big noon meal included two kinds of pie and sometimes cake as well. Devil's food cake was my favorite, along with a huge slice of apple pie. Ma cut her pies into five pieces. "Nobody wants one of those skinny pieces of pie the restaurants serve," she said. The meals the neighborhood women served to the threshing crew were comparable to Thanksgiving dinner; indeed, they were a thanksgiving celebration for a good harvest.

By the time farm boys in our neighborhood reached thirteen or fourteen, they wanted to demonstrate that they were men, and threshing days were a good time to do it. Pitching bundles into the threshing machine proved to be one of the most difficult tasks. With a three-tine fork, the bundle pitcher tossed bundle after bundle into the machine, spacing them so they didn't overlap but allowing no gaps between bundles, either. It took skill and practice to pitch bundles properly. If you worked too hard at it, you tired and had great difficulty pitching off an entire wagonload. But the machine never stopped, so there were no breaks to ease a tired muscle or even to swab a sweaty brow. When you pitched bundles, you kept pitching, no matter what. The entire operation of the machine depended on how well you did it. If you overlapped bundles, the machine growled and slowed down, and the drive belt from the tractor to the thresher began slapping. The same thing happened if you tossed in a bundle crosswise. Each bundle had to be placed straight, with the oat heads going into the machine first.

Part of the knack of bundle pitching was eye-hand coordination: you spotted a bundle, thrust your three-tine fork into it just at the level of the twine band, lifted, and tossed all in one motion. While you were sticking your fork into the bundle, at the same time you were looking ahead for the next one, as there was no time for searching. As a bundle pitcher you became a human perpetual motion machine, never stopping: thrust, turn, pitch, repeat. And you had to keep things level on the bundle load as well. If you stood in one place, allowing bundles to pile high on one part of the wagon, the bundles might fall off, and someone would have to pitch them back on the wagon for you— a major embarrassment.

Pa and the neighbor men watched us kids work. They didn't say anything, didn't say if we were doing the job right or wrong. They didn't have to. We had other ways of knowing. If the tractor's "pom, pom, pom" continued along evenly, without an increase or decrease in volume; if the machine hummed along with all of its belts and pulleys turning effortlessly; if straw flew out the straw pipe onto the straw stack evenly and not in clumps, and men carried bags of threshed oats one after the other without looking up, without looking at you, then you knew you were doing the job well.

THRESHING MACHINES

For hundreds of years people threshed grain by hand, usually with a flail—a wooden stick, often hickory, connected to a handle by a piece of leather. The operator pounded the stick against the grain, which had been spread out on a wooden threshing floor. The threshing floor was in the center section of a three-section barn designed for the storage of wheat, oats, barley, or rye—whatever grain crop the farmer grew. On each

Horsepower sweep threshing in Springwater, Wisconsin, circa 1890 (WHI IMAGE ID 31820)

side of the threshing floor was another bay for storing the grain. These early one-story barns, often called three-bay threshing barns, were common in New England and then in the Midwest as grain production moved into Ohio, Indiana, Illinois, Wisconsin, and Iowa.

The threshing floor of the three-bay threshing barn had big doors on each side that allowed the wind to easily blow through. Once the grain kernels were separated from the straw and chaff, the farmer raked away the straw and tossed the grain kernels and chaff into the air so the wind would blow off the chaff.

Some farmers walked their horses or oxen over the grain on the threshing floor to separate the grain kernels from the straw and chaff. But most farmers agreed that using a flail, although it was much harder work, threshed the grain better than having animals walk over it.

These primitive threshing approaches continued in many parts of the country until the 1850s and in some places well past the end of the Civil War. But inventors had been working on mechanical threshing machines as early as the mid-1700s. A Scotsman, Michael Menzie, is credited with one of the early water-powered machines, invented in 1732, little more than several flails beating on the grain. Another Scotsman, Andrew Meikle, invented a more practical threshing machine in 1788. This machine, also water-powered, included a conveyor to clean the grain.[1]

Several other inventors worked on developing a practical threshing machine, and these early models had one thing in common. They were stationary, which meant the farmer brought his grain to where the thresher was located. Waterwheels powered some of them, but many operated with four to eight

THRESHING MACHINES

teams of horses hitched to a sweep. The Pope thresher was one of the first reliable machines developed in the United States. Manufactured in Boston in the 1820s, it was small and hand operated and thus had minimal capacity for threshing. But the machine did a good job, even though cranking it proved to be harder work than wielding a flail. A treadmill powered by one horse soon replaced the man with the crank. The operator placed the treadmill into a pit he'd dug in the ground, so the horses walked on an incline. The arrangement reminded some of an animal digging into the ground. Soon the machine was called the groundhog thresher.[2]

While inventors worked on various versions of threshing machines, farmers continued to cut their grain with cradles. When Cyrus McCormick invented the reaper in 1831, grain could be more easily and more quickly harvested, and farmers began planting more acres. With more acres, of course they had many more sheaves of grain to thresh. Farmers wanted a better way to thresh their crop.

Brothers Hiram and John Pitts of Winthrop, Maine, began custom threshing with a groundhog machine in the 1830s. By 1837 they had a patent on a more advanced type of thresher that could thresh up to one hundred bushels a day, using a two-horse treadmill for power. The machine was portable and could be moved from farm to farm.[3] The Pitts brothers helped usher in the tradition of the threshing crew, a group of neighbors who went from farm to farm to assist each other with threshing the grain harvest.

J. I. Case did much to advance the development and manufacture of threshing machines. Case, a New Yorker, was born in 1819. Early in his life he developed an interest in threshing machines, and while still in New York, Case worked on improving the groundhog threshers that were somewhat popular at the time. Case set out for Wisconsin's Racine County in 1842. In Rochester, Wisconsin, he continued improving on the groundhog model by adding a fanning mill, meaning the grain could be threshed and cleaned in one operation. He had wanted to build a manufacturing plant in Rochester, but the government officials would not grant him water rights for a factory. So he moved to Racine, where he rented a small factory and began producing threshing machines. By 1847 he had constructed a three-story threshing machine factory called Racine Threshing Machine Works.

The Pitts brothers held some of the patents for Case's threshing machine improvements, but Case didn't hesitate to purchase patents or obtain rights to manufacture. By 1850 a Case Thresher complete with a two-horse treadmill was available, ranging in price from $290 to $320.[4]

By 1860 Illinois led the nation in wheat production, followed closely by Wisconsin. With the manpower shortage brought on by the Civil War, McCormick's reaper began selling more rapidly. Few men were available to swing the still-popular cradle in the grain fields. And the grain had to be threshed. The Case manufacturing plant was located near the emerging wheat fields of Wisconsin and

(continued on next page)

THRESHING MACHINES

(continued from page 149)

Illinois. The demand for Case threshing machines continued to rise.

With the Civil War came the expansion of railroads and telegraph service. Transportation and communication enhanced the operations of companies such as J. I. Case. Now farmers could order farm equipment via telegraph and have the equipment delivered for pickup at their local railway depot.

In 1869 Case offered an improved thresher called the Eclipse. It had an advanced system for moving both straw and grain kernels through the machine. That same year Case began selling a portable steam engine to power its newly remodeled thresher. No longer did farmers have to rely on several teams of horses walking in a circle to provide power for the threshing machine. Steam engines had many advantages over horses: they didn't tire, and they didn't require rest stops during hot weather. Threshing changed once more. Now a steam whistle and the chug-chug sound of the steam engine added to the hum and rattle of the threshing machine.

By 1876 steam traction engines—the forerunner of today's farm tractor—began appearing. Although huge, these ponderous beasts, with steel wheels and a cast-iron frame, not too different from a small steam locomotive, could be driven down the road toting a threshing machine behind.[5] By 1886 J. I. Case was the world's premier manufacturer of steam engines.[6]

Perhaps nothing scared a thresher operator more than fire. A small stone or a piece of metal might inadvertently be tossed into the machine and cause a spark. Occasionally the threshing machine, which was largely constructed of wood, burned to the ground. Wooden threshing machines did not withstand weather well, either. In 1904 Case offered an all-steel threshing machine, solving both problems.[7]

Threshing machines continued to be used as late as the 1950s, when field combines began replacing them. After about 1920, many of the steam engines were replaced by tractors with internal combustion engines. Horses, however, continued to pull bundle wagons for threshing throughout the Depression years and in some parts of the country through World War II and some years beyond.

NOTES

1. Robert N. Pripps, *Threshers* (Osceola, WI: Motorbooks International, 1992), 23–24.

2. Jerry Apps, "History of Threshing Machines," *Country Ways and Country Days* (Stillwater, MN: Voyageur Press, 2005), 57–60.

3. Pripps, *Threshers*, 25–28.

4. C. H. Wendel, *150 Years of Case* (Iola, WI: KP Books, 2005), 5–8.

5. Ibid., 8–9.

6. "Case IH History," www.caseih.com.

7. Pripps, *Threshers*, 55.

There was no greater feeling than the one you had after you unloaded your first load of bundles, backed the team and bundle wagon away from the machine, and stopped by the pump house for a drink of well water. Your shirt was soaked with sweat, and sweat trickled into your eyes. Your arms ached, and your back felt like it did when you handled oak logs all day. But you felt great. You had passed the test.

Nobody said anything to you about what you'd just done. But everyone knew it. You could see it in their faces—especially your pa's face. It was a proud look, a "My kid did that" look.

Soon you headed the team back out to the oat field for another load. You could rest your tired arms and back a little as you slowly made a new load of bundles, with the field pitchers tossing the bundles up to you, one after the other. You soon learned that carefully piling the bundles on the wagon would pay off when you unloaded. You could learn this only from doing it. No one had any guidelines, no suggestions on how to make a load of bundles, just as no one had any directions for pitching off a load. Each person had his own way, had his own style, and developed his own rhythm for doing it. Nobody cared how you did it as long as the threshing machine operated properly and the job got done.

The next day you were on your way to the next neighbor for another round of bundle loading and unloading, big meals, and tall tales. Outside of the meals, the stories were the best part of threshing, stories told every year about bundle pitchers who didn't pass the test, about snakes tossed onto loaded wagons, about wet grain plugging up threshing machines, about horses running away. One story I heard year after year involved a runaway when the threshing crew was at Frank Kolka's farm in the early 1950s. Jim Kolka, Frank's son, told it this way:

We had three teams hauling bundles from the field. Toward the end of the day, we were working on one of the last fields. The bundle wagon drivers were competing to see who could haul the biggest load of bundles. The men operating the threshing machine were waiting for the next load; they were glancing up the lane to the oat fields. The lane wound its way up a steep hill back of our barn.

Jerry York was coming down the lane on that steep hill with a huge load of bundles on his wagon. The horses were straining to hold back the load when the front wooden standard on the bundle wagon [the upright support] broke. Luckily, Jerry fell off to the ground on the side and was clear of the wagon. He had let go of the lines, so the horses ran wild down the hill, scattering oat bundles along the way.

The thresher men saw the runaway team charging down the hill, directly toward the threshing machine. Bill Miller, one of the thresher men, took a three-tine fork and took a swing at the runaways and turned them into a high-wheel wagon that was parked nearby. The impact knocked down the team. The horses had also broken the tongue on the bundle wagon. The men around the threshing machine got the team standing, unhitched them from the wagon, and settled them down. The horses were not hurt. By this time, Jerry came running down the lane, all out of breath, but uninjured. That was the end of his day. He walked his team home.

Meanwhile, the threshing crew unloaded the remaining oat bundles from the broken wagon. After they unloaded the next wagon that came in from the field, they picked up the bundles scattered along the lane. What it all amounted to is, threshing was delayed just long enough so the crew had another meal at Kolka's.[3]

Leo Walsh, an Iowa farm boy, remembers a time when his team ran away when the group was threshing at his home farm:

My job was to drive the team on a bundle wagon, which brought bundles from the oat field to the threshing machine. Our farm was the last stop for the threshing machine as it made the rounds of the neighbors who were yet to combine their grain. We were working on the last field to be threshed. The field was three-quarters of a mile from the farm buildings.

I couldn't get the team to do more than a slow walk out to the field. Coming back, all they wanted to do was run. It was the last load of the day, around five in the afternoon; I had on a really big load of bundles. The team wanted to run, so I thought "you sons of guns, you run." I even helped them out a little bit. For the last eighth or so of a mile I started pulling back on the reins because the driveway was coming up. But there was no stopping them. They had the bits set in their mouths. They ran into our yard at a full gallop. They knew where they were supposed to be going. So they turned a bit trying to get between the threshing machine and the windmill. Well, they didn't quite make it. The front left corner of the wagon rack hit the windmill tower head on. The windmill was relatively new. It was a nice windmill. Worked well. It was forty feet high, able to pick up any available wind.

When the bundle rack hit the windmill, it put a bow in the windmill support of maybe three feet, so the top of the windmill began leaning. Dad stuck his head out of the barn where he had been forking straw. When he saw what happened, he yelled, "Get those horses and wagon away from that windmill."

The threshing crew ran a safe distance and stood watching the leaning windmill. Three or four minutes later the windmill came crashing down. It was the biggest heap of scrap iron I had ever seen.

Dad kept me and my brother busy for several days cleaning up the mess. The wagon was close enough to the threshing machine so the bundles could be unloaded. Dad was usually patient and didn't get too upset. But that was the end of windmills—we didn't get another one. He used the event as an excuse to dig a new well that was deeper and resulted in better water.

At supper that night, Dad said to me, "Maybe you should think about going to college." One of my brothers is still working the home farm.[4]

(Leo Walsh became a professor of soil science at the University of Wisconsin–Madison, and then dean of the College of Agriculture and Life Sciences at the UW.)

Silo Filling

With grain harvesting completed, the last grain bundle threshed, and the threshing machine moved on to another neighborhood, we experienced another brief lull in farmwork. It was mid- to late August. If we'd had regular rains, the corn had been growing and by now was well tasseled and eared out—which meant armlike ears stuck out from the sides of the cornstalks, sometimes two on a stalk. The corn, especially hybrid corn, was usually more than six feet tall. Sometimes when the city cousins would visit the farm, we'd play hide and seek in the corn. Our intent was to lose them in our twenty-acre cornfield. And we did. We'd wait a while for them to yell and then help them find their way out of row upon row of cornstalks, each row looking just like the next. (If you're lost in a cornfield, the secret is to follow a row to its end, which of course will take you out of the field. City cousins seemed to lack this basic knowledge.)

Pa started cutting corn for the silo in early September with a corn binder pulled by Frank and Charlie. The corn was green and growing, and the corn kernels were far from ripe. Corn kernels go through several stages as they ripen: milk stage, dough stage, early dent, and finally dent stage. Sweet corn is in the milk stage when we eat it. For silage, most farmers, including my dad, preferred the corn to be in the dough stage, when it was green enough (had enough moisture content) to pack well in the silo.

Silage is a fermented product; the cut pieces of corn, stalks, kernels, tassels, and leaves are packed tightly to exclude air and encourage fermentation caused by the natural yeasts on the corn plant. Fermentation of corn with too much moisture (kernels in the milk stage) results in a nearly black and poor-tasting silage. Corn with too little moisture (kernels in the dent stage) does not pack properly, resulting in mold and another unpalatable result. So the corn for silage must be cut at exactly the right time. Pa determined this by tearing back the leaves on several cobs of corn to see maturity of the kernels.

We began cutting corn by greasing and repairing our McCormick corn binder and hooking up the team. Horse-drawn corn binders bore some resemblance to grain binders, as they cut cornstalks and bound them into bundles. Corn was planted in rows,

A farmer operates a horse-drawn Milwaukee corn binder, circa 1910.
(WHI IMAGE ID 59945)

SILO FILLERS (ENSILAGE CUTTERS)

By the 1870s Wisconsin was changing from a wheat-growing to a dairy state, and farmers looked for new sources of cattle feed. Wisconsin winters are long and cold, and for a cow to produce milk throughout the winter she needed an abundant source of nutritious feed. Wheat-growing farmers often had a few head of milk cows, but most allowed them to go dry during the winter months. Now farmers who had begun to depend on milk cows for their livelihood reasoned that cows, with proper feeding and care, would produce milk during more than the warm months. Silos could provide another winter source of feed.

Claims for the first silos in the United States go back to 1865, when a farmer in Troy, New York, built one of stone. He apparently used it for just one year because he was disappointed with the results. Levi Gilbert, a Fort Atkinson, Wisconsin, farmer, is credited with building the first silo in Wisconsin, in 1877. It was an underground silo, six feet deep, twelve feet wide, and thirty-two feet long.[1]

Silos and corn silage immediately became controversial. Some cheesemakers refused to buy milk from farmers who fed corn silage, believing the milk was contaminated and would not make good cheese. Some farmers claimed a silage-fed cow would lose its teeth, or its stomach would be eaten away. One farmer claimed silage made his cows drunk, causing them to stagger around the barnyard.[2]

The fact remained that cows needed feed in the winter, and dry hay, although important, could not provide all the nutrition necessary to keep a cow

Farmers fill a silo with a tractor-powered silo filler, or ensilage cutter, 1923. The silo filler cut the corn into about half-inch pieces and blew them up the long filler pipe into the silo, where the material fermented and became silage. (WHI IMAGE ID 23657)

milking at a high level. Farmers slowly began building silos; the first ones were underground and called trench silos, and later ones were upright.

Corn silage requires the corn be chopped into small pieces and packed in an airtight container for fermentation to occur. The fermentation process is anaerobic, meaning no air can be present; if there is air present in the mix, molds develop, and the silage spoils. Machines for cutting the green corn, stalks, leaves, and ears soon appeared. Early ensilage cutters

(continued on next page)

SILO FILLERS (ENSILAGE CUTTERS)

(continued from page 155)
included an elevator mechanism to transfer the chopped cobs and stalks into a silo. But as silos became taller, elevators could not do the job. The next generation of ensilage cutters used a blower and metal pipes to move the cut corn to the top of the silo, where it fell inside.

Starting in the late 1800s, several manufacturers began making ensilage cutters. In 1898 the Appleton Manufacturing Company of Batavia, Illinois, made an ensilage cutter with an elevator. The ad for Appleton's

International Harvester's 1914 catalog of ensilage cutters
(WHI IMAGE ID 23494)

"New Hero" machine proclaimed, "Our universal swivel carrier runs at any desired angle, and can be changed from one angle to another without stopping the cutter."[3] The Silver Manufacturing Company of Salem, Ohio, advertised, "Ohio Ensilage Cutter. Largest capacity, easiest feed, lightest running. Four to 20 tons ensilage per hour blown into highest silo with only four to 15 horsepower."[4]

Several Wisconsin manufacturers made ensilage cutters, including J. I. Case of Racine and Gehl of West Bend. After World War II, tractor-powered forage harvesters, which cut the standing corn into small pieces and blew it into a trailing wagon, began appearing. Once the wagon was loaded, it was mechanically unloaded into a machine that blew the cut material through a long pipe into the silo. This new technology eliminated the corn binder, the silo filler, and of course the silo-filling crew, as farmers could cut and fill their silos by themselves.

NOTES

1. Norman Fish, "The History of the Silo in Wisconsin," *Wisconsin Magazine of History*, December 1924, 161–162.

2. Jerry Apps, *Barns of Wisconsin* (Madison: Trails Books, 1995), 109–112.

3. *Farm Journal*, August 1898, 192.

4. *Farm Journal*, August 1907, 345.

and the early corn binders cut one row at a time. The corn binder had two snouts, which moved on each side of the corn row, steering the corn plant to the knives that cut off the stalks.

Pa hired a man with a silo-filling machine, or ensilage cutter, which cut cornstalks and cobs into half-inch pieces and blew the cut material up a metal pipe into a door at the top of the silo. Pa would not begin cutting corn until he knew exactly the day the man with silo filler would arrive, and he would phone the neighbors to help, as he had done for threshing. A couple days before filling silo, Pa cut corn all day, allowing the green bundles to dry on the ground.

On silo-filling day, the silo filler, which had been put in place against the base of the silo the previous day, awaited the loads of corn bundles to arrive from the fields. Similar to grain harvesting, a neighbor with a team and wagon would drive to the cornfield and stack bundles of green corn on the wagon. Green corn bundles were heavy—many times heavier than grain bundles. So the corn bundles were hoisted onto the wagon by hand, lifted by the twine that wrapped around the bundles.

The teamster drove the load of bundles up to the silo filler, which had a metal conveyor that fed the bundle of corn into the machine. A Farmall H tractor powered the filler, which was one of the noisiest machines to come to the farm. The machine's blower roared, and the cut material rattled as it was blown up the metal pipe to the top of the silo. Only those farmers with teams that would not spook from loud noise helped with silo filling.

Usually by suppertime the silo was full, and hungry people streamed into the house for the second of two meals Ma prepared.

Pa always made sure he had enough corn for a load or two of extra bundles. The next morning, we'd hitch Frank and Charlie to our bundle wagon and run these loads through the machine to refill the silo after the silage had settled several feet overnight. To avoid dangerous silo gas, one of the products of fermentation, Pa would always run the silo filler for a few minutes before feeding in the corn bundles, forcing fresh air into the silo, before anyone entered to pack the fresh silage all around the silo.

With the silo filled, we looked forward to harvesting ripe corn. This would not happen until October, after the corn had ripened and the first hard frosts had turned the green and growing plant brown and ripe.

9

AUTUMN HARVEST

I have fond memories of October on the farm. Cool crisp days. Frosty mornings. Trees turning to many shades of red, yellow, orange, and brown. Canada geese winging over in long Vs stretching from horizon to horizon. The mile walk along the dusty road to our country school. Eating a bright red apple picked from a tree.

I also have memories of the hard work that was involved with corn harvesting, and of less-than-pleasant weather. Late fall days were often cold, raw, and windy. Once the corn was cut, the cornfields became vast, open areas where the weather could get at a person full force. There was no place to hide, nowhere to get out of the wind. But we all knew that the fall work must be completed, because winter waited just around the corner, sometimes making its appearance earlier than we anticipated. The threat of an early winter assured that we took the autumn harvest seriously. Those who didn't finish harvesting corn before the first snows arrived found harvest work considerably more difficult.

Harvesting Corn

We grew about twenty acres of corn, sometimes thirty acres during World War II when Pa fed as many as one hundred pigs. Pigs eat a lot of corn, especially during the weeks we prepared them for market.

Each afternoon upon arriving home from school, I hitched the team to the wagon and headed for the cornfield. By hand I snapped ears of ripe corn off the stalks and tossed them into the wagon. When I had a full load, I drove into the pigpen and threw the ears where the ever-hungry hogs could begin devouring the yellow kernels. I did this every day for much of October.

Before corn binders, corn pickers, and combines, many farmers picked their corn by hand. Growing up in the 1940s on a farm in Missouri, Vern Elefson helped his dad pick corn by hand, with their team pulling the wagon. He recalls one year when they were working in a cornfield badly infested with cockleburs. To keep the burs from matting the horses' tails, Elefson's father tied a white cotton feed bag over each horse's tail.

Later they could remove the burs from the bags much more easily then extracting them from the tails.

The plan seemed to work well. Elefson and his father drove the team to the field, headed them down the row, and began picking corn ears and tossing them in the wagon box. The horses moved along contentedly, gleaning tidbits from the cornstalks. It was November, and no flies buzzed around, so there was no reason for the horses to switch their tails.

They had picked corn for about an hour when for some reason one of the mares switched her tail. As Elefson said, "The result was a strange white object, visible to the backward-seeing eyes of the horses, suddenly jumping at them from behind. The team didn't wait to investigate. They began running across the field as fast as they could, dragging the nearly filled wagon with them."

They didn't run far. At the edge of the field was a thicket of saplings six or eight feet tall. The horses ran straight into them, the saplings bending under the wagon. That stopped them. A neighbor passing by on the road found the incident rather amusing. Later he told the Elefsons, "I had no idea those old mares could move that fast."[1]

Before corn binders and corn shredders, farmers picked corn by hand with a team and a wagon. In this 1927 photo, a farmer picks corn in a cornfield damaged by a windstorm that likely made it impossible to use a corn binder.

(WHI IMAGE ID 46973)

CORN BINDERS

For many years farmers grew much more wheat than corn. Grain, especially wheat, was a cash crop for many pioneer farmers in the Midwest. Corn, on the other hand, was a feed grain, fed to the cows, hogs, and poultry. Farmers sold little corn for human consumption.

Farmers considered cornstalks to be of limited value; they mostly wanted the yellow-kerneled cobs. Some farmers fed cornstalks to cattle and used them for bedding as well. But they saw little feed value in dried cornstalks once the ears had been removed.

Once the corn kernels had turned yellow and the cornstalks became brown and dried, the farmer drove the team and wagon to the cornfield. The farmer walked along the row of ripe corn, grabbed an ear, snapped it from the stalk, and tossed it into the wagon. Corn wagons had one side higher than the other, so when the person picking corn tossed the ear toward the wagon it hit the high board (called a banging board) and then dropped into the wagon.

On most midwestern farms, handpicking corn in the field was the popular approach to harvesting the crop throughout the 1800s and well into the 1900s. By the early 1900s cornhusking contests were a competitive spectator sport. Thousands of people gathered near a big cornfield to watch men and a few women compete to see who could strip the husks off the cobs fastest. The contests were timed, with the winner husking the most pounds of corn in twenty minutes. Of course the corn had to be picked clean, with no husks remaining.

After World War II mechanical corn pickers replaced handpicking, although cornhusking contests continue to this day.

Once farmers determined the cornstalk and leaves, in addition to the ears, had some feed value, they began cutting the entire plant. At first farmers cut corn by hand with a knife. Because corn plants can be as thick as or thicker than a man's thumb, a sickle or scythe was not heavy enough to do the job. Local blacksmiths provided a simple remedy by making a heavier knife, similar to today's machete, that had a heavy straight blade about eighteen inches long and a wooden handle. Later, an improved corn knife had a curved serrated blade about a foot long with an eighteen-inch handle. The operator grabbed a stalk of corn with the left hand, sliced it off near the ground with the right hand, gathered the stalk in the crook of the left arm, and went on to the next stalk. This continued until the number of cornstalks in the arm was large enough to make a bundle. Then the farmer reached around to grab a piece of bundle-length binding twine. The farmer wrapped the twine around the bundle, dropped it to the ground, and went on to the next stalk. The process was slow and tedious. Working steadily, a person could cut and bundle about one acre a day.

The first mechanical horse-drawn corn binders began appearing in the late 1800s, prompted by the acceptance of silos and the storage of chopped, green corn. The D. M. Osborn Company, in 1890, began manufacturing a mechanical corn binder,

(continued on next page)

CORN BINDERS

(continued from page 161) followed by the McCormick Company.[1] By the late 1800s McCormick had considerable experience manufacturing reapers and grain binders. Although grain binders and corn binders were quite different machines, both had a binding mechanism that tied a length of twine around the cut material, forming a bundle.

Horses pull a corn binder, 1914. The binder's large wheel, called the bull wheel, powered the machine via a series of gears. (WHI IMAGE ID 44693)

By the end of World War II, mechanical corn pickers pulled by tractors began appearing. The corn binder was left in the shed or parked under a tree to rust. Once more the dried cornstalks remained in the fields, as the mechanical pickers snapped the ears from the stalks, husked them, and elevated them into a wagon pulled behind the picker. The tractor-powered mechanical corn picker eliminated several tasks: cutting the corn, standing the bundles in corn shocks, and hauling the corn shocks to a corn shredder, which husked the corn.

Similarly, the grain combine, which became popular about the same time, eliminated binding, shocking, and threshing grain. Both the mechanical corn picker and the grain combine made work easier for the farmer. But they also eliminated two important community social events, threshing day and corn shredding day, when neighbors gathered to help each other with the harvest. Threshing and corn shredding gatherings included storytelling, good food, abundant teasing, practical jokes, and the rest of what ties a community together and makes it more than merely a collection of farmers living in the same area.

NOTES

1. J. Brownlee Davidson and Leon Wilson Chase, *Farm Machinery: Practical Hints for Handy-men* (Guilford, CT: The Lyons Press, 1999), 157.

On most farms, by the time a boy was ten or twelve years old he was driving horse-drawn farm equipment, including implements as large as corn binders. Here a young man operates a McCormick corn binder. (WHI IMAGE ID 45050)

My pa would hitch our team to the corn binder and begin cutting the cornfields by mid- to late October, depending on the weather. The corn binder cut the dried cornstalks more easily than it did the green corn for the silo, and thus the team had an easier task. The cooler fall days also made pulling the corn binder a bit easier for the horses.

Once a cornfield was cut, we gathered the corn bundles and stood them into corn shocks. Shocking corn was entirely hand labor, but it was not nearly as disagreeable as shocking oats. Of course we had to bend over to pick up the corn bundles. They were heavier than oat bundles, but we could stand when building the shock. We stood enough bundles in the shock so it would withstand a stiff wind, yet not so many that the bundles on the inside couldn't dry well. We wrapped a length of binder twine around the shock just below the tassels to help keep the cornstalks standing. Our corn shocks looked like teepees, narrow at the top and wide at the bottom, lined up across the stubbled cornfield in neat rows stretching for eighty rods (a twenty-acre field was eighty rods long and twenty rods wide) in a twenty-acre field. It was an artistic creation, yet our sore backs and aching arms didn't allow we boys to appreciate the beauty before us. Pa appreciated what he saw, though; he appreciated the practical and the aesthetic, the economic and the artistic of a field of corn shocks drying under a bright autumn sun with our woodlot, ablaze in fall color, serving as a backdrop.

The next step in corn harvesting in the days before mechanical corn pickers and modern-day corn combines involved husking and shredding the cornstalks. The mechanical corn husker-shedder, designed to perform these two functions, looked somewhat like a threshing machine. The operator moved it from farm to farm, where it was set up and powered by a movable belt attached to a tractor. The machine included a feeding apron; snapping rolls, which removed the corn ears from the stalks; husking

CORN HUSKER-SHREDDERS

In the late 1800s, when farmers began valuing both the kernel-filled cobs and the dried stalks, the need for a machine to separate the cobs from the stalks emerged. A few years earlier, farmers had slowly begun accepting silage and silos, realizing they needed to provide their dairy cattle a source of nutritious, palatable feed throughout the winter months. Making silage required cutting the green corncobs and stalks. Now these same farmers looked for ways to salvage the dry stalks as well.

Farmers generally did not own their husker-shredders but instead relied on a custom operator to come into the neighborhood to do the work, in a manner similar to threshing machines.

Somewhat like a threshing machine, a corn husker-shredder, called merely a corn shredder by many, removed the husks from the corn ears and then shredded the remaining cornstalks into pieces that could be blown into a barn or onto an outside stack.

A few of the earliest models had no husking mechanism and merely shredded the dried corn. But the majority of the machines both husked the cobs and shredded the stalks.

Several machinery manufacturers made husker-shredders. The Appleton Manufacturing Company of Batavia, Illinois, advertised four different sizes of Appleton Corn Huskers: "Will do more and better work than any other machine of like character and corresponding size."[1] Other popular makers of husker-shredders included the Rosenthal Corn Husker Company of Milwaukee, the J. I. Case Company of Racine, and International Harvester Company of Chicago.

NOTES

1. *Farm Journal*, October 1907, 424.

Once the corn was cut and the bundles shocked to dry, they were hauled to the farmstead and fed into a husker-shredder, which separated the cornstalks from the cobs, as seen in this 1905 photo. The cob corn was then stored in corncribs for later feeding. The farmer used the cornstalks for cow feed and bedding in the barn. (WHI IMAGE ID 45182)

rolls, which stripped the husks from the ears; and a shredding mechanism that cut and shredded the stalks and leaves into small pieces.

Corn shredding required a crew of neighbors to help, similar to threshing and silo filling. Drivers with teams hauled loads of cornstalks—they took apart the corn shocks—to the husker-shredder machine. One person fed the corn bundles, butt end first, into the machine; before that the twine was cut on each bundle so the stalks would move loosely through the shredder. The ears of husked corn ran up a chain-driven elevator and dropped into a wagon. Every hour or so, depending on the quality of the corn crop, Pa hitched the team to the wagonload of ears and pulled it alongside the corncrib, where he and another neighbor forked the ears through the roof of the corncrib.

Meanwhile, the machine's blower pipe blew the shredded cornstalks into the barn's hayloft. Pa would feed the cornstalks to the cattle (in addition to hay and corn silage) and also use the stalks for bedding.

It usually took a couple days to complete the corn shredding. A custom operator ran the machine and moved from neighbor to neighbor until all the corn in the neighborhood had been shredded. All but one neighbor's, that is. Albert Davis harvested his corn the old-fashioned way. He and his son, Bernard, cut their corn with corn knives, shocked it, and then throughout the winter used their team to haul the corn shocks to the haymow of their barn. There Albert and Bernard husked the corn by hand, using husking pegs (a metal finger that fit over one's hand) to help strip the cornhusks from the ears. I remember seeing Albert and Bernard in their cornfield on a snowy day in January, chopping the snow and ice from their corn shocks with an ax so they could load them on their wagon. As long as they farmed, into the 1960s, they harvested their corn as farmers had since colonial days.

With the potatoes in the bin and the corn in the corncrib, we'd completed the fall harvest. Now we looked to several months of easier times, but surviving winter was always a battle, especially in the Upper Midwest. Cutting, hauling, sawing, and splitting wood seemed never ending and became our next challenge.

10

THE QUIET SEASON

When we'd forked the last cob of corn into the corncrib and the corn shredder lumbered on down the road, the planting-growing-harvesting season officially ended. It was November, the days shorter, the nights colder, and the first flakes of snow appearing. The horses at our farm, tied in their warm stalls at the end of the cow barn, had little to do other than to pull the manure spreader half a mile to the field and back or, when the snow got too deep, pull a sleigh through the barn each morning when the gutters were cleaned. The rest of the day the horses stood in their stalls, resting, eating hay, and putting on a little weight, since pulling the manure spreader or sleigh once a day was easy work compared to what was expected of them during the rest of the year.

One winter Pa and a Wild Rose village blacksmith and welder, Jim Colligan, invented a sleigh with a dump box for hauling manure. We called it Pa's chariot.

Pa's homemade manure-carrying sleigh saved many hours of work, but I believe he also enjoyed the trip to and from the cornfield each morning. Frank and Charlie, with little work to do in winter, were frisky and walked with their heads high. Pa, riding high on the chariot, drove them down the snow-packed country road to the field, the sleigh runners squeaking on the cold snow. He turned into the field, sometimes smashing through snow drifts four feet high. The team enjoyed the challenge, and Pa savored the ride.

Once in the field, Pa climbed off and pulled a lever on the chariot, and the box filled with manure tipped up, allowing the load to slip to the ground, forming a little pile. Then it was back home, with the horses trotting along the country road that saw even less traffic in winter than in summer, other than the milk hauler and the mail carrier. Of course, the manure had to be hauled every day, including Christmas and New Year's.

During these long winter days, morning and evening chores continued, but when we got home from school in the afternoon we had time for hunting and, as soon as the lakes froze to sufficient depth, ice fishing. However, making wood filled many of our winter days. We heated our farmhouse with woodstoves, one in the dining room and one in the kitchen. We also kept a woodstove going in the pump house and in the potato cellar—a total of four ever-hungry wood burners.

Making wood included several tasks, none of them especially appealing. We cut dead oak trees from the twenty-acre woodlot that was just to the north of the farm buildings. Once a tree was down, we sawed off the limbs and cut the trunk into six-foot lengths. When this part of the work was finished, and it might take several days, Pa hitched the team to the bobsled, and we headed for the woods. The bobsled consisted of four wooden runners with heavy wooden crosspieces between each pair, plus a hitch and tongue for the team. Metal strips were fastened to the bottom of each runner. Local blacksmiths in our part of Wisconsin made bobsleds for farmers. They sawed the runners, turned up in the front, from white oak pieces three inches by ten inches by five feet long. With Frank and Charlie pulling, our bobsled could haul as many limbs as we could pile onto it. We hauled the limbs to a place near the farmhouse where we stacked them in an enormous pile, six feet or so tall and sometimes a hundred feet long. To tote the larger logs, Pa wrapped a logging chain around each one, and the team pulled them through the snow to the limb pile, one at a time. With little else to do at this time of year, the horses seemed to enjoy working in the cold and snow, much more than I did, to be sure.

Winter trips to town were often made with a team and a bobsled.

(WHI IMAGE ID 43377)

THE JACKRABBIT AND THE CHARIOT

After one of Pa's daily sleigh trips on the manure spreader, he returned to the barn excited because he had seen a big jackrabbit sitting under some bushes at the edge of the field. In those days, the fencerows were a tangle of shrubs and trees, mixed with piles of stones we had removed from the field in previous years. A jackrabbit is several times larger than a cottontail, weighing more than ten pounds and about two feet long. In winter they are pure white with black at the tips of their ears. In summer their fur is brown. And they can run up to forty miles an hour.

Hunting season for jackrabbits was still open. Pa asked me to hold the team while he ran to the house for his shotgun. Soon he returned, out of breath, carrying his double-barrel 12-gauge. He climbed into the back of the slippery chariot, which only a brief time ago had been loaded with manure, and trotted the team back to the field. The jackrabbit had not moved. Pa steered the empty sleigh as close as he could without fear of spooking the rabbit. He quietly said, "Whoa" to the team and put the harness lines between his knees. He pulled back both hammers on

the 12-gauge and took careful aim. A sharp *kaboom* broke the morning silence. Hearing the loud report, Frank and Charlie immediately spooked and took off galloping across the snow-covered field. Pa slipped on the sleigh's floor and fell, covering himself with slick manure. He managed to keep the reins as he steered the frightened runaways around and around the field, the snow flying and the chariot nearly tipping on some of the turns. After three or four rounds, the team tired enough so Pa could control them, but they wouldn't go near where he had shot the jackrabbit.

He drove the team home, a broad smile across his face. He was covered with manure from the top of his woolen cap to the tip of his six-buckle rubber boots.

"What happened to you?" I asked.

"Got me a jackrabbit," he said. "Big one, too."

While I unhitched the team from the chariot and led the horses into the barn and unharnessed them, Pa walked back to the field for the rabbit. It was the largest jackrabbit we had bagged all hunting season.

Our team and bobsled had other winter uses besides toting wood from the woodlot. When winter storms shut down our road, which occurred several times each winter, we hauled our ten-gallon cans of milk with the team and bobsled to the nearest plowed road.

Arland McKittrick, who grew up in Crawford County, Wisconsin, recalls one winter when the snow was so deep the milk hauler couldn't make the rounds of the farms to pick up milk. McKittrick loaded his cans of milk on a bobsled, picked up his neighbors' milk, and hauled the load to the highway, which had been cleared. "The milkman met us there and took the milk the rest of the way to the cheese factory," McKittrick remembers.[1]

No matter how deep the snow or how low the temperature, a team and bobsled could make it through. The day my twin brothers were born, January 31, 1938, proved how important that could be to a rural family. In those days, babies were born at home, as for many the nearest hospital was more than forty miles away. Usually a midwife assisted, along with a doctor (who made house calls in those days).

The day before my brothers were born a fierce blizzard swept across central Wisconsin, shutting down the country roads. The snowplows, still fairly primitive, attempted to keep the state and county roads open but didn't even try to clear the connecting roads until the storm died out. Luckily we did have a telephone in those days. When it became clear my brothers were on their way, Pa called the doctor in Wautoma, some twelve miles away. Pa agreed to meet the doctor at the intersection of our country road and the county trunk road, which had been plowed. Pa drove the team and bobsled and had an ample supply of blankets and quilts.

With the doctor in the sleigh, Pa turned toward home, stopping at the Millers' place to pick up Augusta Miller, the neighborhood midwife. They all arrived safely at our farmhouse, and later during that long, snowy, and extremely cold night, my twin brothers came into the world.

The years when we grew twenty and more acres of potatoes and stored them under the house and in the potato cellar, Pa hauled potatoes to the potato buyers in Wild Rose with the team and the bobsled in late February or March, on a day when the temperature was above freezing. We removed the box from the steel-wheeled wagon and fitted it on the bobsled, where we could pile up to a ton of sacked potatoes. On the front of the bobsled we placed a "sleigh coop," a little wooden building with a big window in front, a door on the side, and little windows on the sides and back. The wagon box served as the floor. A small sheet metal stove with a stovepipe stood in the corner of the sleigh coop opposite the door. A slot for the harness lines was cut under the big window. With a fire in the little stove, the teamster driving the bobsled was as comfortable as if he was back home sitting by the kitchen cookstove.

Potato prices skidded to their lowest shortly after the fall harvest as many farmers sold their potatoes then rather than store them. Because we had a potato cellar with a woodstove, Pa stored our potatoes hoping the prices would rise as winter wore on. During the Depression and World War II years, potato warehouses lined the Chicago and Northwestern Railway tracks in Wild Rose. As potato growing had become a major cash crop for many small dairy farmers in central Wisconsin, almost all of the small towns with railway access had potato dealers and potato warehouses. Potato dealers owned the warehouses and bought potatoes from farmers, stored them briefly in their

A WINTER HORSE STORY

My father grew up in Adams County. He told a story about my grandfather hauling potatoes to a nearby warehouse on a cold, blustery day in the 1920s.

Grandpa was headed for Plainfield, the nearest railhead in those days, with his team and bobsled loaded with potatoes. The road to Plainfield was crooked and snow covered, and the snow was blowing, making visibility difficult. As he drove along, Grandpa heard someone singing church hymns—the sound carried well on a cold day. He found a fellow standing in the middle of the road, next to his team and bobsled, singing.

"What's the matter?" Grandpa asked.

"Broke the evener pin on my sleigh." (The evener connected the horses to the sleigh.)

"You got an ax with you?" Grandpa asked.

"Yeah, I do,"

"Lend me it, and I'll cut you an oak pin."

Grandpa found an oak tree nearby, cut a crude pin, and shoved it into the evener, temporarily fixing the sleigh.

"By the way," Grandpa asked. "Why were you singing church hymns?"

"I was singing for God to come, and he came."

"I sure as hell ain't God," Grandpa said, and he drove off, shaking his head.

warehouses, and then shipped them south and east, to Chicago, St. Louis, Cleveland, and eastern cities.

Pa kept track of the market, and usually by mid-January he was dickering with the potato dealers for a good potato price. It became a bit of a trade-off. Our ever-hungry woodstove in the potato cellar consumed piles of wood. Keeping the fire going—especially when the temperatures regularly slid to ten, twenty, sometimes thirty degrees below zero—became a daily chore. Yet Pa wanted the best price possible for his potato crop. To complicate the situation further, potatoes could not be hauled long distances with a team and sleigh when the temperature hung around zero. They would freeze in less than half an hour exposed to that kind of weather.

With the potato prices up, Pa waited for a January thaw when the temperature climbed above thirty-two degrees for a few days. From the middle to the end of January, Pa kept an eagle eye on the weather, watching the sunsets and sunrises, feeling the air—these were the days before weather forecasts. We knew when we woke up to meltwater dripping from the farmhouse roof that Pa was ready to bag and haul potatoes. A potato sorter, a machine turned with a hand crank, separated the smaller potatoes from the larger ones and transported the larger ones to a slot where Pa had attached a burlap bag. Each bag held one hundred pounds of potatoes. We weighed each bag of potatoes before

Pa stitched the bag shut with a huge needle and binding twine, ending up with two tufts of burlap like ears sticking up on each side of the bag's top. These served as handles for moving the bag, one person on the bottom of the bag lifting, the second person holding onto the burlap handles. The bags were tossed into the sleigh box and covered with old blankets and quilts Ma had discarded. Pa hitched the team to the sleigh, fed the lines through the slot under the sleigh coop window, and headed off to Wild Rose to sell our potatoes.

We sorted, bagged, and loaded as long as the weather held and the temperature didn't dip back to below zero. Usually in a couple of days we had emptied the potato cellar and could breathe a little easier.

With the potatoes sold, we now looked forward to the remaining days of winter, filled with school, daily chores, ice fishing, rabbit hunting, skiing, and sledding. I don't recall Pa ever hitching the team to the bobsled for recreational purposes such as a winter sleigh ride. For him the bobsled and the team were strictly used for work, not for play.

Stored above the potato cellar, along with other farm machinery, was our cutter. This was a fancy sleigh, usually pulled by one horse and used for going to town or visiting neighbors. The inside of the cutter was lined with red velvet, and it had ornamental doors that opened with little brass latches. My brothers and I often sat in the cutter, imagining we were driving a horse down a snow-covered road. But in my memory, we never used the cutter.

In the early 1900s those who owned cars often put them up on blocks—jacked them up and put wooden blocks under the axles—after the first snowfall. These people depended on their horses for transportation, as they had before the arrival of the first autos. Those who owned fancy cutters used them for social visits, going to church, and grocery shopping in town. Those who couldn't afford cutters depended on their horse-drawn bobsleds to haul them where they wanted to go. Community sleigh rides, sometimes sponsored by the church or 4-H Club, were wonderful social experiences. A bobsled pulled by a spirited team of horses, with an ample supply of fresh straw and warm blankets, offered young and old alike a pleasant break from the routine of winter.

With more available time, farmers also used the winter months to repair broken harnesses, to oil them and polish them and make them ready for another season. Sometimes the repairs were more complicated than a farmer could do, so the local harness shop was called into action. There the harness maker, a skilled leather craftsperson, made whatever repairs were necessary, or in some cases made new equipment such as a bridle or a halter.

Country people used cutters primarily for trips to town, visiting friends, and traveling to church. This photograph was taken in Eagle River, Wisconsin, in 1902.
(WHI IMAGE ID 59545)

Farmers often used large bobsleds like this one for sleigh ride parties in addition to the more utilitarian tasks around the farm.
(WHI IMAGE ID 48032)

Many farmers took on other jobs and activities during the winter months. Art Swan of Shell Lake, Wisconsin, recalls some of this extra work:

> *Two of my brothers took a job in a logging camp near Loretta, Wisconsin. They hauled logs with a team and helped ice the roads at night so it was easier to haul big loads. They drove the horses home in the spring, following the railroad tracks from Loretta. They had two of dad's teams in the logging camp.*
>
> *As I grew up, I skidded logs for loggers many times. My brothers and I were skidding logs off a steep hill one time. There was about three feet of snow. One of my brothers chained a log behind one horse and sent him down the hill with the log by himself. I was on the bottom of the hill. I unhooked the log and sent the horse back up the hill. We kept doing that with two horses and got those logs down the hill the easy way.[2]*

Some farmers also used their teams to help with clearing snow, before motorized snowplows became popular. Swan recalls, "About 1927, my brother went to Siren, Wisconsin, where he worked for the township. One thing he did was operate a homemade snowplow that worked off side of a horse-drawn sleigh. It took eight horses to pull the sleigh with snowplow attachment."[3]

By the first of March, all of us—Pa, Ma, my two brothers, and I—eagerly waited for the coming of spring and a repeat of the farming seasons. I suspect Frank, Charlie, and Dick, our farm horses, looked forward to spring work as well. Even for horses I'll bet loafing gets a little old after a few months of it.

Farm life is a cycle, always dependent on seasonal change and the weather. It all begins with a flurry in spring; it ends quietly with the coming of winter. In between, during the planting, haying, and harvesting seasons, farmwork is never ending, often from dawn to dark. A farmer's life is filled with predictable events, yet it is ever changing. And the horses, like the farmers who drive them, seem to look forward to each new challenge of the changing year.

During the winter some farmers made extra money by hiring out to loggers and skidding logs out of the woods. Here loggers use horses to haul a huge log in Cable, Wisconsin, 1904. (WHI IMAGE ID 53490)

OLD WORLD WISCONSIN HISTORIC SITE / WISCONSIN HISTORICAL SOCIETY

NOTABLE EVENTS IN AGRICULTURE *

1701: Jethro Tull, England, invents the first practical grain drill. For centuries farmers have sown grain seeds by hand. It will be many more years before most farmers use grain drills.

1732: Michael Menzie, Scotland, develops a simple, water-powered threshing machine. It is stationary, with farmers hauling their grain to the machine for threshing.

1797: Charles Newbold, New Jersey, patents a cast-iron plow, but it meets resistance from farmers who believe the iron will poison the soil.

1812: Peter Gaillard, Pennsylvania, invents a grass-cutting mower. For many years grass for hay has been cut with a sickle or a scythe. It will be many more years before farmers routinely use horse-powered mowers.

1814: Jethro Wood, New York, patents a plow with movable parts. If one part breaks, it can be replaced without replacing the entire implement.

1822: Jeremiah Bailey, Pennsylvania, patents an improved grass-cutting mower.

1825: The Erie Canal opens from Buffalo to Albany, New York, allowing a market route from the Middle West to the East. It also provides a ready route for immigrant travel to the Great Lakes and then on to such states as Michigan, Minnesota, and Wisconsin.

1831: Cyrus McCormick, Virginia, develops and uses a reaper on his home farm. He will not patent the machine until 1834, causing a host of future problems.

1833: John Lane, Illinois, invents a steel plow for heavy midwestern soils. The plow, made from a saw blade, develops a shiny surface and soil does not stick to it.

1833: Obed Hussey, Maryland, is granted a patent for a reaper.

1834: Cyrus McCormick receives a patent for a reaper, six months after Hussey, but claims his (McCormick's) patent should have preference because of his 1831 reaper history.

1837: John Deere, Illinois, begins manufacturing steel plows, and they quickly become popular with midwestern farmers, allowing the company to grow rapidly.

1837: Brothers Hiram and John Pitts, Maine, patent a threshing machine that threshes up to one hundred bushels a day, using a two-horse treadmill for power. It is portable and can be moved from farm to farm.

1839: Percherons are the first draft horse breed imported to the United States from Europe.

1840–1850s: Railroads become popular and expand the American frontier.

1842: J. I. Case, a New Yorker, moves to Rochester, Wisconsin, and begins manufacturing threshing machines. Moving to Racine in 1843, Case becomes the largest manufacturer of threshing machines in the world and the first to construct them of steel in 1904. He also becomes known as the first American to create a steam engine for agricultural use.

1847: William F. Ketchum, Buffalo, New York, invents a hay mower designed specifically to cut hay. Earlier ones were combination reapers and mowers.

1847: Cyrus McCormick moves his reaper manufacturing business to Chicago. His brothers, William S. and Leander J., are in business with him.

1850s: Kerosene lamps and lanterns become popular, replacing candles as light sources.

1851: George Brown, Illinois, patents a horse-drawn corn planter.

(WHI IMAGE ID 11836)

1852: H. L. Emery, New York, begins manufacturing stationary hay presses, forerunners of present-day hay balers.

1853: Walter Abbott Wood, New York, invents a functional dump rake.

1856: C. A. McPhitridge, Missouri, invents a device for tying wire around a grain bundle.

1858: Charles W. and William W. Marsh of Dekalb, Illinois, patent the Marsh Harvester (reaper). They claim their harvester will cut an acre of grain in less than an hour.

1860s: Illinois and Wisconsin lead the nation in wheat production.

1860: George and Daniel Van Brunt, Wisconsin, invent a combination grain drill and cultivator.

1862: Morrill Land Grant College Act passes, establishing agricultural and mechanics colleges across the country.

1862: Homestead Act passes, turning over 270 million acres of public domain land to private citizens. The law will remain in effect until it is repealed in 1976.

McCORMICK'S HARVESTER AND TWINE BINDER.

1862: The United States Department of Agriculture is established but does not receive cabinet status until 1889.

1867: William Louden, Iowa, invents a practical hay carrier for unloading hay in barns. Now loose hay can be moved from wagon to haymow mechanically, allowing for larger barns and an easier haying season for farmers accustomed to pitching hay into the barn with a three-tine fork.

1870s: Silos for the storage of winter feed become popular. By 1950 Wisconsin will have 137,194 silos.

1873: William Deering of Maine moves to Illinois and begins managing a company making Marsh grain harvesters. By 1890, the Deering Harvester Company will be a major competitor of the McCormick Harvester firm.

1874: Joseph Glidden, Dekalb, Illinois, patents barbed wire.

1877: J. S. Kemp patents a manure spreader with a movable apron.

1878: John Francis Appleby, Wisconsin, patents a device that ties grain bundles with twine. Grain binder manufacturers quickly adopt Appleby's invention to replace wire-tie machines.

1880: William Deering, Chicago, secretly manufactures binders with the Appleby knotter. They immediately sell. Deering Harvester Company in Chicago grows rapidly.

1890s: Several machinery manufacturers begin making ensilage cutters, used to cut green corn stored in silos to become silage, a new product for winter feeding of dairy cattle.

1890: Stephen Moulton Babcock, University of Wisconsin, develops a machine to test the butterfat content of milk. It provides a way of paying farmers for their milk and discourages those who cheat and dump water in their milk.

1896: Rural free delivery begins (RFD). Farmers now have mail delivered to their farms.

1900: Farmers begin using telephones. However, by 1950 only about half of the farmers in Wisconsin will have a telephone.

1902: The McCormick Harvester Company, the Deering Harvester Company, the Plano Manufacturing company, and two smaller firms merge to form International Harvester. By 1910, International Harvester will employ 17,000 workers in the Chicago area and will be one of the leading industrial corporations in the United States.

1920: Enclosed gear tractors begin to appear.

1930s: Tractors with rubber tires become available. Because of the Great Depression, many farmers continue using horses because they cannot afford tractors.

1936: President Franklin D. Roosevelt signs the Rural Electrification Act (REA), which helps thousands of farmers receive electricity. Unfortunately, because of World War II, many farmers will not have electrical power until the middle 1940s.

*Adapted from *Yearbook of Agriculture 1940* (Washington, D.C.: United States Department of Agriculture, 1940), 1184–1196.

EMPLOYED PEOPLE WORKING ON FARMS IN UNITED STATES *

1790: 90 percent of employed people

1820: 83 percent

1840: 77.5 percent

1870: 47.4 percent

1900: 34.7 percent

1910: 33.2 percent
13.6 million workers, 6.4 million farms

1920: 26.3 percent
13.4 million workers, 6.5 million farms

1930: 21.5 percent
12.5 million workers, 6.5 million farms

1940:
10.9 million workers, 6.35 million farms

1950:
9.9 million workers, 5.6 million farms

1960:
7.0 million workers, 3.9 million farms

1970:
4.5 million workers, 2.9 million farms

1980:
3.7 million workers, 2.4 million farms

1990:
2.9 million workers, 2.1 million farms

2000:
2.8 million workers, 2.1 million farms

*From National Agricultural Statistics Service, "Number of Farms and Land in Farms," "U.S. Number of Farms and Farms Workers 1910–2000," www.nass.usds.gov/Data_and_Statistics.

A boy rides on a horse-drawn corn binder, circa 1905. (WHI IMAGE ID 45218)

NOTES

Part 1

1. Robb Sagendorph, ed., *The Old Farmer's Almanac Sampler* (New York: Ives Washburn, Inc., 1957), 150.

Chapter 1

1. Robert West Howard, *The Horse in America* (Chicago: Follett Publishing Company, 1965), 247.

2. Juliet Clutton-Brock, *Horse Power: A History of the Horse and the Donkey in Human Societies* (Cambridge, MA: Harvard University Press, 1992), 11–15.

3. "Story of Farming," www.historylink101.com/lessons/farm-city/story-of-farming.htm.

4. Frances Haines, *Horses in America* (New York: Thomas Y. Crowell, 1971), 90.

5. Richard N. Current, *The History of Wisconsin, Volume II, The Civil War Era, 1848–1873* (Madison: State Historical Society of Wisconsin, 1976), 58.

6. Charles Josiah Galpin, *Rural Life* (New York: The Century Company, 1918), 35.

7. Ibid., 35–36.

8. National Park Service, U.S. Department of the Interior, "The Homestead Act," Homestead National Monument of America, www.nps.gov/archive/home/homestead.

9. The International Museum of the Horse at Kentucky Horse Park, "The Draft Horse in America: Larger Farms Need Greater Horsepower," www.imh.org/museum/ drafthorse.php?chapter=4.

10. Ibid.

11. Howard, *The Horse in America*, 251.

12. Everett E. Edwards, "American Agriculture—the First 300 Years," *Farmers in a Changing World*, Gove Hambidge, ed. (Washington, DC: United States Department of Agriculture, House Document No. 695, 1940), 232.

13. Jerry Apps, *The People Came First: A History of Wisconsin Cooperative Extension* (Madison: Wisconsin Cooperative Extension, 2002), 10.

14. American Society for the Prevention of Cruelty to Animals, "About Us/History," www.aspca.org/ about-us/history.html.

15. "Wisconsin Agriculture in Mid-Century," *Crop Reporting Service Bulletin* 325 (Madison: Wisconsin Crop and Livestock Reporting Service [no date]), 42.

16. Howard, *The Horse in America*, 169, 170.

17. Apps, *The People Came First*, 9.

18. Ibid.

19. *Farm Journal*, March 1893, 72.

Chapter 2

1. Material from Carl W. Gay, *Traditional Horse Husbandry* (Guilford, CT: The Lyons Press, 2003), 84–100, and E. H. Hughes, "Horses and Mules," in Frank D. Gardner, *Traditional American Farming Techniques* (Guilford, CT: The Lyons Press, 2001), 573–578.

2. *Farm Journal*, July 1898, 165.

3. Ibid.

4. Susan McBane and Helen Douglas-Cooper, *Horse Facts* (New York: Barnes and Noble Books, 1993), 31.

5. Lynne R. Miller, *Work Horse Handbook* (Sisters, OR: Small Farmer's Journal, Inc., 2004), 79–93.

6. Carl W. Gay, *Traditional Horse Husbandry* (Guilford, CT: The Lyons Press, 2003), 247.

7. W. C. Fair, *The People's Home Stock Book* (Cleveland, OH: R. C. Barnum Company, 1910), 3.

8. Ibid., 4.

9. Howard Peck, personal correspondence, September 8, 2006; Joyce Peck Soholt, personal correspondence, September 9, 2006.

10. Walter Bjoraker, personal correspondence, January 15, 2006.

11. "McKallor Drug Company, Binghamton, NY," *Farm Journal*, April 1911, 265.

12. Dr. J. Robert Curtis, interview, Portage, WI, March 15, 2007.

13. Ibid.

14. Ibid.

15. Jim Erb, interview, Lake Mills, WI, September 7, 2006.

16. McBane and Douglas-Cooper, *Horse Facts*, 42–43.

17. The International Museum of the Horse at Kentucky Horse Park, "Settling the American West: Horse Related Crafts and Industries," www.imh.org/museum/ history.php?chapter=80.

18. Jerry Apps, *Ringlingville USA* (Madison: Wisconsin Historical Society Press, 2004).

19. Sears, Roebuck and Co., 1908 Catalog, 121.

20. Mary Bellis, "The History of Horseshoes," www.inventors.about.com/library/inventors/blhorseshoe.htm.

21. "Drove 2,000,000 horseshoe nails," *Merrill Herald*, May 5, 1921.

22. Sears, Roebuck and Co., Spring and Summer 1940 Catalog, 918.

Chapter 3

1. Robert West Howard, *The Horse in America* (Chicago: Follett Publishing Company, 1965), 251.

2. Brenda Kruse, "The Green Girl weekly web column," February 25, 2002, www.bleedinggreen.com/GG2002.html.

3. *Farm Journal*, March 1907, 137.

4. Studebaker Company, www.studebakermotorcompany.com/history.

5. *Farm Journal*, February 1911, 105.

6. Dictionary of Wisconsin History, Wisconsin Historical Society, "Carriage and Wagon Industry in Wisconsin," www.wisconsinhistory.org/dictionary.

7. *The History of Racine and Kenosha Counties* (Chicago: The Western Historical Society, 1879), 547.

8. www.stoughtonlandmarks.com.

9. *Farm Journal*, June 1898, 148.

10. Dr. J. Robert Curtis, interview, Portage, WI, March 15, 2007.

11. W. C. Fair, *The People's Home Stock Book* (Cleveland, OH: R.C. Barnum Company, 1910), 269.

12. Ibid.

13. "The Days before Yesterday," *Draft Horse Journal*, February 1966, 15.

14. Jerry Apps, *Ringlingville USA* (Madison: Wisconsin Historical Society Press, 2004).

15. Gary B. Nash, et al. *The American People: Creating a Nation and a Society* (New York: Harper Collins, 1996), 505.

16. Robert C. Nesbit and William F. Thompson, *Wisconsin: A History* (Madison: University of Wisconsin Press, 1989), 480, 482.

17. Jerry Kronschnabel, personal correspondence, September 15, 2006.

18. Vern Elefson, personal correspondence, September 18, 2006.

19. Give Us a Home, "Horses: Frequently Asked Questions," www.giveusahome.co.uk/horses/faq.htm.

20. Howard Sherpe, "Across the Fence," *Westby Times*, March 5, 2007.

Chapter 4

1. Orin Schleicher, interview, Mount Morris, WI, September 2, 2006.

2. Hidden Springs Creamery, www.hiddenspringscreamery.com.

3. Baldur Farm, www.baldurfarm.com.

4. *Rural Heritage*, www.ruralheritage.com.

5. Palmquist Farm, www.palmquistfarm.com.

6. Olson Cenury Farm, www.wildwebranchers.com/olsoncenturyfarm.

7. *Rural Heritage*, www.ruralheritage.com/logging.

8. Noma Petroff, "To tell the truth—This country is not going to survive without draft horse power," *Small Farmer's Journal*, Winter 2006.

9. Ken Laing, "Horse Power for Organic Farms, *Rural Heritage*, www.ruralheritage.com; used with permission.

10. Roy Reiman, *Horse Power* (Milwaukee: Reiman Publications, 1977), 11–40.

11. *Draft Horse Journal*, www.drafthorsejournal.com/features/horsepulling/horsepulling.htm.

12. www.horsepull.com/results/Michigan/2008/Hillsdale.dwt.

Chapter 5

1. Jim Erb, interview, Lake Mills, WI, September 7, 2006.

Chapter 6

1. Art Swan, personal correspondence, October 20, 2006.

2. Robert C. Nesbit, *The History of Wisconsin, Volume III: Urbanization and Industrialization, 1873–1893* (Madison: State Historical Society of Wisconsin, 1985), 39.

3. Edgerton Tobacco Days, Inc., "Edgerton's Heritage Days," www.tobaccoheritagedays.com/heritage2.htm.

4. Clarence Olson, personal correspondence, March 5, 2007; Howard Sherpe, *Across the Fence* (Madison, WI: Prairie Viking Press, 2006), 91–93, 165–167.

5. Charlie Sweet, personal correspondence, August 15, 2006.

6. Vern Elfeson, personal correspondence, August 19, 2006.

7. Orrin Schleicher, interview, Mt. Morris, WI, September 2, 2006.

Chapter 8

1. *Farm Journal*, March 1898, 75.

2. Clarence Olson, personal correspondence, March 5, 2007.

3. Jim Kolka, interview, Wild Rose, WI, September 2, 2006.

4. Leo Walsh, interview, Madison, WI, March 6, 2006.

Chapter 9

1. Vern Elefson, personal correspondence, August 16, 2006.

Chapter 10

1. Arland McKittrick, personal correspondence, September 5, 2006.

2. Art Swan, personal correspondence, October 14, 2006.

3. Ibid.

INDEX

Page numbers in **bold** refer to illustrations.

(PHOTO BY STEVE APPS)

ABOUT THE AUTHOR

Jerry Apps is professor emeritus at the University of Wisconsin–Madison and the author of several books on rural history and country life. Jerry's nonfiction books include *Old Farm, Every Farm Tells a Story, Living a Country Year, When Chores Were Done, Humor from the Country, Country Ways and Country Days,* and *Ringlingville USA.* His historical fiction includes *In a Pickle* and *Blue Shadows Farm.* He received the Council for Wisconsin Writers' 2007 Major Achievement Award and the Wisconsin Library Association's 2007 Notable Wisconsin Author Award.

Jerry was born and raised on a small farm in Waushara County, Wisconsin, where he grew up farming with horses. As a small boy he learned from his father to treat horses as a part of the family, to care for them, respect them, and work with them as he would with any other family member.

PRAISE FOR *HORSE-DRAWN DAYS*

"This book depicts not only the farmer's love for his horses; it also describes the entire farming process that was in place when horse power wasn't what was under the hood."
Joan Sanstadt, News Editor, *Agri-View*

"In *Horse-Drawn Days*, Jerry provides a good mix of history, information, and the storytelling that his fans have come to appreciate. The book offers information about work horses that might otherwise be lost if it wasn't written down. It was an important time in our history, and there aren't that many people who can remember those days. And there especially aren't many people who can tell the story as well as Jerry Apps."
Jim Massey, editor, *The Country Today*

"A historical narrative showcasing not only the value of the horse as a result of its contributions to the survival of rural farmers, but also underlining its valuable role as a member of the farm family."
J. Liv Sandberg, Equine Extension Specialist, Department of Animal Sciences, University of Wisconsin–Madison

"The vital details that have gone into *Horse Drawn Days* are just another example of Jerry Apps's precise attention to detail. The stories woven in with all these details help even people with no connection to the land or agriculture enjoy the work. Personally, it was a little shocking even to me—a farm girl—how much change agriculture has gone through in such a short period of time! It makes one wonder what the next fifty to seventy years will look like. It also better helps me understand the deep appreciation some of my family members have for their draft horse stories."
Pam Jahnke, Farm Director, Farm Report Radio

"An accurate and highly readable history of the big-hearted animals who partnered with our forebears in feeding the nation . . . from the gentle giants who hauled the plows to the plucky light horses that drew the family buggies to town. The book is plumb full of useful information as well as inklings that may well serve our future."
Annie Randall, owner, Village Booksmith, Baraboo, Wisconsin, and longtime Morgan horse breeder